Machiavelli
A Beginner's Guide

Cary J. Nederman

ONEWORLD
OXFORD

A Oneworld Book

Published by Oneworld Publications 2009

ISBN 978-1-85168-639-1

Typeset by Jayvee, Trivandrum, India
Cover design by www.fatfacedesign.com
Printed and bound in Great Britain by TJ International

Oneworld Publications
185 Banbury Road
Oxford OX2 7AR
England
www.oneworld-publications.com

Learn more about Oneworld. Join our mailing list to
find out about our latest titles and special offers at:

www.oneworld-publications.com

For Edward J. Whetmore

Nihil facile est

Contents

Preface

Niccolò Machiavelli has been among the most closely studied and the most widely debated figures of modern Western thought. Every year, dozens of scholarly books and articles, not to mention popular introductions and adaptations, appear in print in all of the major European languages. Translations and editions of all of his works abound. The logical question, then, is why yet another survey of Machiavelli's thought is justified, given this already crowded field. My answer is relatively simple. Most book-length accounts of Machiavelli's ideas, advanced as well as introductory, fall into one of two categories. One group of studies tends to concentrate on his two major and best-known political treatises – *The Prince* and the *Discourses on the First Ten Books of Titus Livy* – to the virtual exclusion of the remaining body of his vast literary output. As one recent scholar, Joseph V. Femia, has insisted with notable candor, none of the writings other than *The Prince* and *Discourses* 'adds anything to our understanding of Machiavelli's thought' (2004, p. 6). The other main approach to Machiavelli narrates his biography without offering any sustained examination and interpretation of the central elements and unifying threads of his thought. While such examinations of his life possess the virtue of covering the range of his corpus, the cogency of his intellectual framework tends to get lost in the morass of biographical exposition and detail.

By contrast, in the following book, I adopt a different path to understanding Machiavelli. Specifically, I integrate both the political and biographical elements employed by previous authors, while also attending to various of his lesser-known writings in order to investigate the progress of his intellectual growth and to identify important continuities in his thought. Much of the scholarship on Machiavelli addresses the dual vexed questions of whether he was an internally consistent and coherent thinker and of whether he was in fact as 'original' or 'innovative' as he sometimes encouraged his readers to believe. In my view, such an approach misses the point. Machiavelli wrote in multiple contexts and for diverse audiences – for republican statesmen and aspiring princes, as well as for popular readers and for intimates – such that rendering a definitive and final judgment on the entirety of his corpus requires inattention to some parts of his literary output. To talk about the 'unity' or 'main principles' of Machiavelli's teaching is to miss the rich and vivid texture of his writings.

My reading of Machiavelli adopts a quite different approach from previous interpretations. For me, his intellectual 'core' emerges less from a commitment to fixed philosophical or theoretical doctrines than from a set of basic dichotomies and contrasts that troubled and guided him throughout his life and to which he returned regularly. These dichotomies include the relationships between the heavens and the earth, between fixed human nature and innovative change, between violence and law, and between security and liberty. Such themes become evident as we examine the range of his writings – prose and poetry, political theory and history, diplomatic dispatches and private correspondence. Of course, in a relatively brief introduction to Machiavelli's thought, it will not be possible to investigate all the details and nuances that helped shape his intellectual vision. But both the enduring questions that exercised his mind and the evolving answers that he gave to them are rendered more transparent by means of a holistic approach to his life and work.

The deeply dichotomized quality that one finds in Machiavelli's writings is replicated, in turn, by the highly divergent interpretations to which they have been subjected. From almost the moment of their publication, his works – political treatises, literary creations, and prose texts – engendered strong and extremely polarized reactions from his readers. Was Machiavelli a 'teacher of evil' or a proponent of republican civic virtue? A trickster or a political scientist? A principled statesman or a pundit? An inveterate liar or a man of his word? A parodist or a stern revealer of painful realities? In my view, the deeply divided reactions of Machiavelli's audience to his writings, from the sixteenth century to the present, reflect the profound dichotomies with which he wrestled and which informed both his life and his literary output. In confronting his main themes, Machiavelli showed a pronounced ambivalence. Human beings seemed to him powerless before supernatural forces, yet also able to overcome external limitations. They appeared constrained by their own natural psychological make-up, but empowered by their ingenious capacity to reshape themselves and to innovate political institutions. They responded to fear and threats of violence, yet could be moved by legal regulation to act for the common good. They craved physical security, but desired to possess freedom and to exercise imperial dominion.

It is probably safe to say that at no time during his career did Machiavelli finally and adequately resolve these tensions. Rather, they continued to trouble him and to stimulate his reflections throughout his life. This, then, forms the 'core' of the Machiavellian project: his unrelenting engagement with contradictions that he could grasp and articulate, but never quite move beyond. Consequently, the organization of the present book represents an attempt to capture and to stabilize for the contemporary reader the primary elements of Machiavelli's worldview. If we seek to identify the essential doctrines or teachings of

Machiavelli, we will be permanently frustrated. If we turn our attention to the contrasts and contradictions that animated and disturbed him, however, we will encounter the complex texture of his thought and the enduring legacy of the quandaries, if not solutions, that he bequeathed to later centuries – ours no less than earlier ones.

Of course, this understanding of Machiavelli may not satisfy readers who want to apply a definitive label to his work, as has been the tendency of most previous scholars. Since, on my account, such final conclusions are not possible, I have presented in this book the textual evidence supporting my approach, derived from the full range of Machiavelli's writings, without entering into direct dialogue with or criticism of preceding interpreters. But it may be useful to highlight a few ways in which my vision of Machiavelli differs from the bulk of conventional scholarship. First, I take seriously Machiavelli's references to supernatural forces and do not judge him to be sacrilegious, impious, or even particularly hostile to fundamental Christian tenets. Moreover, I do not find him to be an exceedingly immoral or amoral thinker, but instead a shrewd student of the human condition as it applies to public affairs. In addition, I view Machiavelli as neither a proponent of monarchy (let alone tyranny) nor an unalloyed defender of republican self-government; while he may have preferred a popular regime, he acknowledged the strengths (as well as weaknesses) of rule by one man. Furthermore, he considered conquest and imperial expansion to be the ultimate goals of politics, but realized the many difficulties posed by the use of military force. Next, from my perspective, Machiavelli was in certain regards highly original, yet he did not break entirely with the past or reject the present, instead mining both history and recent events for many fruitful lessons. Finally, his writings demonstrate considerable intellectual consistency over the course of his career, although his ideas clearly developed and matured over his lifetime and, to some extent, in response to his experiences. In stating these claims at the outset, I hope to make evident, without entering into extended academic debate, the basic features that differentiate my interpretation from the many other readings that are available.

Acknowledgements

Machiavelli has long been a source of fascination for me, going back to my days as a seventeen-year-old, first-year undergraduate at Columbia University, when one of my first essays in a core curriculum Western civilization class addressed the relationship between ethics and politics in his thought. I would not have begun to undertake the current project, however, if I had not received encouragement in its early phases (starting in the late 1980s) from such generous scholars as Marcia Colish, Bettina Koch, and Russell Price. And I could never have produced a finished manuscript if I had not been pushed very hard to do so by Leah DeVun, Susan Dudash, and, once again, Marcia Colish. For assistance in the composition of specific chapters, I am indebted to Jennifer Willyard, Tsae Lan Lee Dow, Tatiana V. Gomez, Mary Elizabeth Sullivan, and Martin Morris. I owe profound thanks to each of these scholars, and I hope any individuals whom I have forgotten to mention, on account of the waning memory that comes with declining years rather than the value of their contributions, will forgive me. I also benefited from the research assistance of my students Christie Maloyed and S. Corby King. Finally, Karen Bollermann must be singled out as a constant source of succor (and sometimes pointed criticism) during much of the time I conceptualized and composed the book.

The opportunity to begin drawing together my meditations on Machiavelli was a Faculty Research Leave granted to me in Spring 2006 by Texas A&M University. My thanks are due to the Head of the Political Science Department, Patricia Hurley, and the Dean of the College of Liberal Arts, Charles Johnson, for supporting my application. Likewise, the Melbern C. Glasscock Center for Humanities Research at Texas A&M, under the leadership of James Rosenheim, has provided a congenial environment in which to engage with my fellow campus scholars. The Political Theory Convocation at Texas A&M – comprising my colleagues Ed Portis, Lisa Ellis, Judy Baer, and Diego von Vacano, as well as a roster of graduate students too large to mention here – afforded me a stimulating (if occasionally heated) venue in which to explore many of the ideas that appear in these pages. My editors at Oneworld, first Martha Jay, who commissioned the volume, and later Mike Harpley, who shepherded it through the editorial process, have been models of support and founts of sage advice.

This book is dedicated to my best and oldest friend, Edward J. Whetmore. Edd has lived a life as varied and whimsical as mine has been single-minded and serious; he has been at various times a disc jockey, advertising copywriter, academic, gambler, union leader, screenwriter and film producer, popular author, and now academic once again. Yet in a friendship that extends over four decades, and many geographical shifts for both of us, we have managed to find sufficient common ground to sustain a close and deep bond. While I doubt that this book will earn sufficient royalties to pay off all of my debts to Edd – metaphorical as well as material – I hope that the dedication will be accepted as a marker. It's never easy, old buddy.

Cary J. Nederman
College Station, Texas

Abbreviations

AMM   Niccolò Machiavelli, 'Allocution Made to a Magistrate,' ed. and trans. A.J. Parel, *Political Theory*, 18 (1990): 525–7.

AW   Niccolò Machiavelli, *The Art of War*, in CW, pp. 566–726.

C   Niccolò Machiavelli, *Clizia*, in CW, pp. 822–64.

CW   Alan Gilbert, ed. and trans., *Machiavelli: The Chief Works and Others* (Durham: Duke University Press, 1965).

D   Niccolò Machiavelli, *Discourses on the First Decade of Titus Livy*, in CW, pp. 188–529.

HFOS   Myron P. Gilmore (ed.), Judith A. Rawson (trans.), *Machiavelli: The History of Florence and Other Selections* (New York: Simon & Schuster, 1970).

MF   James B. Atkinson and Daniel Sices, eds and trans., *Machiavelli and His Friends: Their Personal Correspondence* (DeKalb: Northern Illinois University Press, 1996).

P   Niccolò Machiavelli, *The Prince*, in CW, pp. 10–96.

1

Politician/author

For a man whose career and writings were to become so widely known and controversial, Niccolò Machiavelli's personal origins were relatively modest and inauspicious. He was born on 3 May 1469 into a once powerful and prestigious Florentine family that had fallen on hard times. His father, Bernardo, had studied law but apparently practiced his profession little or never. Rather, the family relied on a small and not especially productive farm for its main source of income, although Machiavelli and his parents and siblings (two older sisters and a younger brother) were probably raised primarily in an ancestral compound, composed of a set of small apartments, in the Santo Spirito quarter of urban Florence. (The farm still stands, but the Machiavelli complex in the city was destroyed during World War II bombing.)

Not a great deal is known for certain about Machiavelli's early life, but the discovery in the mid-twentieth century of his father's diary (more a notebook of accounts and possessions) gives us some idea of his daily circumstances. Bernardo quite clearly struggled to make ends meet and was constantly burdened with debt, which gave him no end of trouble. Most usefully for us, he recorded in his diary his acquisition of printed books and manuscripts, for despite his economic straits he was an inveterate collector and accumulated a library that, while small by contemporary standards, was substantial for someone of his means. All told, he mentions twenty-seven volumes in his library, some of which he purchased, while others he borrowed. Given his training as a lawyer, it is unsurprising that many of these were legal tomes – both books of classical Roman law and works of more recent vintage, including an expensive edition of Gratian's masterwork of church (canon) law, the *Decretum.* He also came to possess translations of and commentaries on Aristotle's writings, as well as a number of Latin classics on history, rhetoric, philosophy, and natural science, either through purchase or on loan. When he could not afford to buy or manage to borrow a volume, he combed libraries to which he was given access or even engaged in bartering his labor to acquire a book (he once indexed Livy's writings for a printer in return for a copy of the volume). Bernardo was evidently an aspiring bibliophile, and his eldest son would naturally have been exposed from a very young age to a wide range of literature as a consequence.

In light of his father's literary aspirations, Machiavelli apparently received from an early date as broad an education as the family could afford, initially from two unknown tutors and then as a pupil of a more renowned Latin teacher, Paolo da Ronciglione. It appears that he attended the Studio Fiorentino (the precursor of the University of Florence), and may have acquired a reputation in his youth for his poetry. Beyond these meager facts, all we have is speculation. Of course, even a cursory glance at his corpus reveals that he received the rudiments of a broad humanistic education in the Greek, Roman, and vernacular classics of poetry and prose typical of the Italian Renaissance. Machiavelli's writings do not assist us very much, however, in recovering the specifics of the curriculum he followed. That he knew most of the important classical Latin authors – rhetoricians, historians, orators, and philosophers – is clear enough from direct or oblique references to them throughout his works. He also shows familiarity with the main philosophers and historians of Greek antiquity (albeit probably in translation), as well as with the major pre-humanists (such as Dante and Petrarch) and humanist authors writing in Italian and Latin between 1300 and 1500.

Political career

It is not until the later 1490s that events in Machiavelli's life become better documented. His mother, Bartolomea (neé di Stifano Nelli), about whom very few facts are known, died in 1496 (Bernardo was to follow in 1500). By this date, his sisters had long been married off and his brother was preparing for the priesthood. Machiavelli himself had probably shifted his focus from his education at the Studio to service at the lowest rungs of the Florentine government, the details of which are not recorded. While clearly a man of some erudition, he thrived first and foremost in the world of public affairs. Once he received appointment as the Second Chancellor of the Republic of Florence in June 1498, we receive a fuller and less speculative picture of his life. The Second Chancery was one of the two central professional administrative bodies of Florence, so that Machiavelli's headship of it placed him at the nexus of political and bureaucratic power. Technically responsible for supporting the elected government of Florence and its leaders in domestic affairs, the Second Chancery in fact overlapped in its activities so greatly with the slightly more prestigious First Chancery (supposedly the diplomacy branch) that by Machiavelli's day there was no evident division of labor between them. The position was not only powerful, it was highly lucrative; all that was required of Machiavelli to retain it (the job had an initial two-year term, with annual reappointment thereafter) was to remain in the good graces of the Florentine government by serving it efficiently. While Machiavelli's selection for the office might seem surprising for a previously obscure civil servant, his distance from the preceding regime of the Medici family, his father's reputation, and no doubt his own networking skills all played important roles.

To appreciate the climate within which Machiavelli's political career was shaped, we need to survey briefly the political

landscape of Italy around 1500. The peninsula was dotted
with dozens of semi-autonomous city states, ruled either by
dynastic clans (such as the Medici family in Florence) or by some
form of self-governing quasi-popular body styled after the traditions of the ancient republics (and especially Rome). These city
states entered into an intricate and ever-shifting set of political
and military alliances and pacts, built around the four 'great
powers' of northern and central Italy: the Duchy of Milan, the
Republic of Venice, the city of Florence, and the Roman
Papacy. The major players on the Italian scene in turn often
depended on the resources of other European states – France,
Spain, and the Holy Roman Empire, most especially – in order
to achieve their strategic goals. Florence had been governed by
a republican constitution since 1494, when the ruling Medici
family and its supporters were driven from power as the result of
a complex set of military and political machinations occasioned
by the invasion of the French king Charles VIII. While the
Florentine Republic initially was under the sway of the charis-
matic preacher Fra Giralamo Savonarola, his execution in 1498
paved the way for a more stable form of self-government to
emerge.

Machiavelli was thrust to the fore as one of the leading
magistrates of the post-Savonarolan republic. In his role as
Secretary, his duties alternated between planning the city's
military strategy and engaging in diplomacy. As a diplomat, in
particular, Machiavelli seems to have excelled. During the next
few years, he traveled widely, representing Florence and her
interests to the major leaders of Italy as well as to the royal court
of France and to the Holy Roman imperial curia of Maximilian.
In his various diplomatic capacities, he observed many of the
famous and infamous figures of early sixteenth-century Europe,
including those (such as King Louis XII of France, Cesare
Borgia, and Pope Julius II) who became central objects of study
in his political works.

The large body of Machiavelli's existing diplomatic corre-spondence, dispatches, and essays of commentary from these early years testifies to the facility with which he handled his delicate political assignments, not to mention his shrewd talent for understanding and analyzing the personalities and institutions with which he came into contact. These writings also provide important source materials that Machiavelli mined as examples for his political reflections in his theoretical writings. We find in them an appraisal of the tactics used by successful governments as well as recommendations for how the political masters of Florence might best ensure the city's safety in the midst of the diplomatic and military posturing of its friends and enemies. From the first phase of his career (1497/8–1502), we also have roughly fifty letters between Machiavelli and his intimate friends, a number that multiplies exponentially in subsequent years. In this correspondence, we encounter the usual reports of daily events that we might expect, but also some insightful reflections on the rough-and-tumble world of politics as he experienced it and on the relation between his personal obser-vations and his education in history and philosophy. Even today, these letters make for fascinating reading.

In between his extensive travels, Machiavelli managed to woo and wed Marietta Corsini, the daughter of a family similarly positioned on the social and economic ladder to his own. Details about this union are obscure, but the marriage seems to have occurred in the second half of 1501. In rapid order Marietta bore Machiavelli a daughter, Primerana, and a son, Bernardo, and eventually five more children, even though he continued to leave Florence for long periods of time on diplomatic missions (and also continued to indulge his widely known penchant for womanizing). How much genuine affection he had for his wife, as opposed to a sense of patrimonial duty to reproduce his dynasty, is an open question, but they remained a couple until his death.

As the sixteenth century dawned, Machiavelli's political star rose even higher into the firmament. In 1502, the Florentine Republic's Great Council authorized a constitutional restructuring that created the executive position of *gonfaloniere* (or chief administrator for life), to which Machiavelli's patron and mentor, Piero Soderini, was appointed. During the following decade, Machiavelli thrived and his influence and prestige grew. Soderini relied upon Machiavelli's advice for a number of political enterprises and added to his authority by appointing him Secretary of two august committees, initially the Ten of War (the Florentine body charged with coordinating matters of the city's relations with foreign powers), and later the Nine of the Militia. In performing these duties, Machiavelli is commonly credited with reviving the Florentine militia as an alternative to the city's long-standing reliance on allies and mercenaries for troops. He pushed this plan and recruited his fellow citizens tirelessly. He also pursued an ambitious (and eventually unsuccessful) plan to redirect the River Arno as part of a Florentine siege of Pisa, an enterprise apparently suggested and designed by Leonardo da Vinci, with whom Machiavelli collaborated closely. Nor did he cease his diplomatic activities, traveling to leading secular courts as well as to the papal curia. One senses that he was a primary source of many of Florence's important initiatives throughout the first decade of the sixteenth century, enjoying the complete trust and backing of his political master, Soderini, even when his ambitious enterprises did not succeed.

At the same time, Machiavelli's growing influence and authority drew him into conflict with some of the leading citizens of Florence. He increasingly engaged in political and personal bickering with those who opposed his plans, including individuals whom he had previously counted among his friends. The evidence suggests that this was not sheer jealousy on their part, but rather that Machiavelli himself did much to alienate powerful men by pushing forward with his own agenda and refusing to adopt a conciliatory attitude toward their objections. Perhaps with his exalted position, his head swelled and he developed what political pundits today call the 'arrogance of power'. Nor did Machiavelli do anything to deflect opportunities for an expanding number of enemies to attack him, especially in regard to his personal affairs. He frequented prostitutes and then bragged of his escapades in correspondence to friends. He likely kept mistresses in the cities to which he regularly traveled. Of course, such behavior was hardly unknown at the time on the part of many persons occupying high office. Still, his open flaunting of sexual conventions made him an easy target – an anonymous accusation forwarded to the Florentine judiciary in 1510 called upon him to be investigated for engaging in anal intercourse with one well-known prostitute – to the point where his friend Giovan Battista Soderini, a nephew of Piero, counseled him not 'to fool around too much' (MF, p. 137). Whatever the merits of the gossip and the charges against him (which were evidently not vigorously pursued by the authorities), Machiavelli came to be regarded with suspicion.

In the event, Machiavelli's political star fell almost as rapidly as it rose. In August 1512, guided by Pope Julius II and with the assistance of Spanish troops, Medici forces defeated the Republic's citizen army and immediately forced dissolution of the government. Machiavelli helped draft Piero Soderini's resignation letter and assisted his former mentor into exile. In turn, Machiavelli himself became a direct victim of the regime change. After having sent several cautionary letters of advice to the returned ruling family, he was removed from his position in the Chancery and placed in a form of internal exile in early November 1512. Worse still, in February 1513, he was imprisoned and tortured for several weeks as a result of (incorrect) suspicions about his involvement in a conspiracy against the Medici. Released a few weeks later when it became clear that he was ignorant of the plot, Machiavelli was forty-three years old and thrust down from the high office that he had so cherished.

Author of *The Prince*

Machiavelli's enforced retirement to his farm outside Florence afforded the occasion and the impetus for him to turn to literary pursuits. The first of his major writings from this period of political exile is also ultimately the one most often associated with his name: *The Prince*. Written during the latter part of 1513 (and perhaps early 1514), but only published posthumously in 1532, *The Prince* was composed in great haste by an author who was, among other things, seeking to regain his status in the Florentine government. (Many who had held office during the republican period were quickly rehabilitated and returned to service under the Medici.) In a letter to his friend and former colleague Francesco Vettori, dated 10 December 1513, Machiavelli describes his composition of 'a short study, *De principatibus*' (referring to the original Latin title of *The Prince*, a common generic term for rule by one man), which sets out to 'discuss what a principality is, how many different types there are, how they are gained, how they are held, why they are lost' (MF, p. 264). Machiavelli denies that its main teachings are directly his own, but instead reflect his gleanings from a nightly imagined 'conversation' among members of 'the ancient courts of the men of old,' who invite him to listen in to their discourses and who even permit their guest 'to ask them why they acted as they did, and out of kindness they respond' (MF, p. 264). In the same letter, Machiavelli debates the pros and cons of presenting the results to the new head of the Florentine wing of the Medici, Giuliano de'Medici. He feared that the book might not be read by its intended audience and would instead fall into the hands of his enemies, who could use it against him. Whether before or after Giuliano's death in early 1516, Machiavelli apparently decided to pursue formal presentation and wrote the letter of dedication that we now possess to the subsequent Medici lord, Lorenzo de'Medici, who almost certainly did not read it when it finally came into his hands.

Scholars have disagreed about whether *The Prince*, in the version that has been bequeathed to us, represents a work that Machiavelli polished and added to throughout his life. Thus, for instance, some have argued the twenty-sixth and final chapter, calling upon the Medici family to unite Italy while driving out the foreign troops housed on Italian soil, constitutes an addition that reflects later events. There are, however, many good reasons to believe that the work was conceived and composed as a totality; certainly, its rhetorical development and logical structure are tightly arranged. Whatever editorial grooming Machiavelli performed on the body of his text beyond early 1514 or so was largely cosmetic.

It is commonplace, and not entirely inaccurate, to say that Machiavelli wrote *The Prince* as a sort of extended job application, a résumé in support of his effort to rehabilitate himself politically. From first to last, he promises to reveal 'hidden knowledge' about how its princely reader might learn to govern successfully (especially as a 'new' ruler) that no other counselor would teach. We know from his letters that almost immediately after he was sacked in 1512, and for the rest of his life, he engaged in a non-stop campaign to return to active service in Florentine government. *The Prince* may rightly be understood as one prong in this pursuit. Yet even after he had finished writing the main part of the treatise, as he expressed in his letter to Vettori, Machiavelli remained ambivalent about whether he should in fact present it to the ruling Medici house. Perhaps he was scared that his ideas were too novel, too extreme, for the audience he envisioned to appreciate.

The Prince, and Machiavelli with it, have stood accused over the centuries of taking a 'cold-blooded', 'cynical', even 'evil', stance about the vicissitudes of politics. The immediate circumstances of its composition perhaps justify Machiavelli in adopting such a tone. Yet the work, although written quickly and in the heat of the moment, is far more complex than a simple characterization suggests, representing the distillation of nearly two decades of political experience as well as the benefits of a solid humanist education. In particular, Machiavelli challenges the common view among political philosophers that there exists a special relationship between moral goodness and legitimate authority. Many authors (especially those who composed mirror-of-princes books or royal advice books during the Middle Ages and Renaissance, a genre that *The Prince* is very carefully designed to satirize) believed that the use of political power was only rightful if it was exercised by a ruler whose personal moral character was strictly virtuous. Thus rulers were counseled that if they wanted to succeed – that is, if they desired a long and peaceful reign and aimed to pass their office down to their offspring – they must be sure to behave in accordance with conventional standards of ethical goodness. In a sense, it was thought that rulers did well when they did good; they earned the right to be obeyed and respected inasmuch as they showed themselves to be spiritually and morally upright.

It is precisely this moralistic view of authority that Machiavelli criticizes at length in *The Prince*. For Machiavelli, there is no moral basis on which to judge the difference between legitimate and illegitimate uses of power. Rather, authority and power are essentially coequal: whoever has power has the right to command; but goodness does not ensure power and the good person has no more authority by virtue of being good. Thus, in direct opposition to a moralistic theory of politics, Machiavelli says that the only real concern of the political ruler is the acquisition and maintenance of power (although he talks less about power per se than about 'maintaining the state'). In this sense, Machiavelli presents a trenchant criticism of the concept of authority (by which is meant the right to rule) by arguing that the notion of legitimate rights of rulership adds nothing to the actual possession of power. *The Prince* purports to reflect the self-conscious political realism of an author who is fully aware – on the basis of direct experience with the Florentine government – that goodness and right are not sufficient to win and maintain political office. Machiavelli thus seeks to learn and teach the rules of political power. For Machiavelli, power characteristically defines political activity, and hence it is necessary for any successful ruler to know how power is to be used. Only by means of the proper application of power, Machiavelli believes, can individuals be brought to obey and will the ruler be able to maintain the state in safety and security.

The political theory contained in *The Prince*, then, represents a concerted effort to exclude issues of authority and legitimacy from consideration in the discussion of political decision-making and political judgment. Nowhere does this come out more clearly than in his treatment of the relationship between law and force. According to Machiavelli, the legitimacy of law rests entirely upon the threat of coercive force; authority is impossible for Machiavelli as a right apart from the power to enforce it. Consequently, Machiavelli is led to conclude that fear is always preferable to affection in subjects, just as violence and deception are superior to legality in effectively controlling them. As a result, Machiavelli cannot really be said to have a theory of obligation separate from the imposition of power; people obey only because they fear the consequences of not doing so, whether the loss of life or of privileges. And of course, power alone cannot obligate one, inasmuch as obligation assumes that the agreement to obey is freely chosen and that one could meaningfully have done otherwise. Consequently, the perspective articulated in *The Prince* stands at some considerable remove from traditional teachings about why people ought to obey law. For Machiavelli, people are compelled to obey purely in deference to the superior power of the state. If a person thinks that he should not obey a particular law, what eventually leads him to submit to that law will be either a fear of the power of the state or the actual exercise of that power. It is power which in the final instance is necessary for the enforcement of conflicting views of what ought to be done; one can only choose not to obey if one possesses the power to resist the demands of the state or if one is willing to accept the consequences of the state's superiority of coercive force.

Machiavelli's argument in *The Prince* is designed to demonstrate that politics can only coherently be defined in terms of the supremacy of coercive power; authority as a right to command has no independent status. He substantiates this assertion by reference to the observable realities of political affairs and public life as well as by arguments revealing the self-interested nature of all human conduct. For Machiavelli it is meaningless and futile to speak of any claim to authority and the right to command which is detached from the possession of superior political power. The ruler who lives by his rights alone will surely wither and die by those same rights, because in the rough-and-tumble of political conflict those who prefer power to authority are more likely to succeed. Without exception the authority of states and their laws will never be acknowledged when they are not supported by a show of power which renders obedience inescapable. The methods for achieving obedience are varied, and depend heavily upon the foresight that the prince exercises. Hence, the successful ruler needs special training in order to acquire the ensemble of qualities that Machiavelli summarizes by the term *virtù*, a word translated variously as skill, wisdom, ability, strength, prowess, and vigor (among other equivalents), which ensures political success in the application of power. *The Prince* proposes to offer the rudiments of such instruction, based on the lessons of history and direct observation of the actual workings of politics.

Although *The Prince* is commonly read as a book of advice about how to rule states, we should not neglect that the larger part of the text is designed to address the problems that stand in the way of acquiring power over a city or territory in the first place. Machiavelli regards this to be the primary challenge facing a 'new prince' (by which he means a ruler who acquires office by his own efforts alone), who is the main audience for his ruminations. In effect, Machiavelli seems to be encouraging the Medici clan to whom the book is addressed to engage in a program of military adventurism. Indeed, when the chapters of *The Prince* are broken down thematically, they reveal more concern for issues of conquest than for difficulties posed by established rule. For example, chapters 1–6 discuss the various types of principalities that one may encounter, including what Machiavelli terms 'mixed principalities'. The latter differ from entirely new principalities in that they occur when a new part has been added on to the existing state. One might infer that Machiavelli suggests that part of one's function, upon becoming the new ruler of a city such as Florence, is to expand the terri- tory at one's command. Without this goal, the discussion of types of principalities and the particular problems they present to a ruler would not seem warranted.

Beginning with chapter 7, Machiavelli turns his attention away from the types of principalities one may encounter and examines the ways in which a ruler might come to power. For example, a prince may gain his position through 'another man's arms and Fortune', by the use of 'wicked deeds', or 'with the aid of his fellow citizens' (P, 7, 8, 9; CW, pp. 29, 35, 39). Machiavelli provides indices of a ruler's strength and makes a special note about the rule of ecclesiastical states. Again, the themes addressed in these chapters suggest the centrality of conquest. Without this vision, Lorenzo and the Medici would surely find these chapters irrelevant because of the family's customary claim, established over the course of the fifteenth century, on dominion over Florence. The victory of 1512 against the Soderini-led Florentine government represented simply the recapturing and renewing of Medici hegemony after a relatively brief republican interlude; the family was already intimately familiar with the city and with the intricacies of civic and regional politics.

In the third thematic section, chapters 12–14, Machiavelli reflects on the types, uses, and composition of armies as well as the role that the prince should play in military affairs. He makes it clear that rulers must think only of military matters and should prepare themselves for war, even during times of peace (P, 14; CW, p. 55). Machiavelli further argues that while it is important for troops to be kept in good shape and well trained, the prince must also submit himself to military preparedness. He advises that the ruler familiarize himself with his own land for two reasons. First, this will allow the prince to defend himself well in the event of an invasion. Second, and more importantly, Machiavelli states that 'by means of his knowledge and experience of such military sites, easily he comprehends the qualities of another other site which he needs to examine for the first time. The hills, the valleys, the plains, the rivers, the swamps of Tuscany, for instance, have a certain likeness to those of the other regions' (P, 14; CW, p. 56). These chapters seem to indicate that *The Prince* was written as a guide for the rule of conquered or annexed territories, not the continued governance of Florence. The Medici simply did not fit the mold of the 'new' ruler which *The Prince* overtly addresses, unless Machiavelli conceives of them as conquerors of new lands, rather than as merely the longstanding heads of the Florentine state restored to power after a brief fling with republicanism.

Nor does Machiavelli's concern with conquest end at chapter 14. He devotes chapter 21, for example, to a discussion of 'how a ruler conducts himself in order to gain high reputation' (P, 21; CW, p. 81) and uses as his primary example Ferdinand of Aragon, the current King of Spain. Like the Medici, Ferdinand does not fit the model of a 'new prince', if by that phrase is meant a ruler who acquires his own state entirely anew. However, Machiavelli insists that he 'may be called almost a new prince because through fame and glory he transformed himself from a petty ruler to the foremost king among the Christians' (P, 21; CW, p. 81). Machiavelli notes that Ferdinand achieved fame and glory throughout his reign, precipitated by his attack on Granada. Machiavelli claims that 'this undertaking was the foundation of his power'. He subsequently attacked Africa and Italy, and invaded France. Machiavelli praises Ferdinand because 'always he performed and planned great actions, which kept the minds of his subjects always in surprise and wonder, watching for the outcome' (P, 21; CW, p. 81). Once again the greatness of the prince is measured not according to his stable maintenance of existing government, but his ability to extend his dominion over lands beyond those he or his family have traditionally ruled.

The crescendo to this argument arrives in the twenty-sixth and final chapter of *The Prince*. Although controversial because Machiavelli changes literary styles in his conclusion and shifts to an emotional plea for the Medici 'to seize Italy and restore and free her from the barbarians', chapter 26 fulfills the general plan of the book. He describes the 'beaten, robbed, wounded, [and] put to flight' condition of Italy; Italians, he says, are 'ready and eager to rally to the banner, if only someone will raise one high' (P, 26; CW, p. 93). The identity of the liberator is none other than Lorenzo Medici (and his family). As Machiavelli argues, there is nowhere Italy 'can turn in her search for someone to redeem her with more chance of success than to your own illustrious house'. Italy cries out to be rid of its foreigners, and God has similarly provided signs that the time is right. As Machiavelli declares, 'Everything has come together to make you [the Medici family] great' (P, 26; CW, p. 94). If Lorenzo takes on the leadership of this adventure, not only could he unify Italy and reap the financial rewards of success, but he would also gain fame, love, and respect for his family. Machiavelli exhorts Lorenzo to visualize the perfect timing of this endeavor, the talents of the Italian people, and the benefits of unification for Italy, Florence, and the Medici.

Author of the *Discourses*

In any event, this ambitious plan did not capture the attention and energy of Lorenzo and his family, and Machiavelli moved on from *The Prince*. Almost immediately after completing *The Prince*, and probably while still refining it, he commenced another writing project that was far more ambitious. This became his other major contribution to political thought, the *Discourses on the First Decade* [or *Ten Books*] *of Titus Livy*. The *Discourses*, as the book is more or less universally known, constitutes an exposition of the principles of republican rule masquerading as a commentary on the work of the famous historian of the Roman Republic, Livy, a volume owned by Machiavelli's father. Unlike *The Prince*, the three books of the *Discourses* were authored over a long period of time (commencing in 1514 or 1515 and completed in 1518 or 1519, although only published posthumously in 1531). The ideas contained in the book may have been shaped by informal discussions that occurred at the Orti Oricellari (gardens owned by the prominent Rucellai family), which were attended by Machiavelli. These conversations, which included some of the leading Florentine intellectual and political figures, enjoyed the sponsorship of Cosimo Rucellai, one of the men to whom Machiavelli dedicated the *Discourses*. During the centuries following their publication, the *Discourses* achieved a readership on par with *The Prince*. Indeed, it seems at least reasonable to suppose that, had Machiavelli never written *The Prince* or had he suppressed it, his achievement as a leading political thinker would have been secured by the praise and defense of republican government contained in the *Discourses*.

The *Discourses* return to the familiar theme of Florentine imperialism, though this time in the guise of a defense of republican expansionism, by inviting the reader to reflect on the reasons for the stunning successes accomplished, in particular, by Rome. As Machiavelli observed, 'We see that cities where the people are in control grow enormous in a very short time, and much more than those that have always been under a prince, as Rome did after she expelled the kings and Athens after she freed herself from Pisistratus.' Indeed, the connection between republics and successful expansion is so strong that it leads him immediately thereafter to declare that 'governments by the people are better than those by princes' (D, 1.58; CW, p. 316). The cause of this is mainly that republics are founded on liberty. And it is for the sake of liberty, Machiavelli believes, that men will pursue glory and exercise *virtù*, Machiavelli's quintessential term for political success. Meanwhile, in places where 'tyranny is established over a free community, not the smallest evil that results for those cities is that they no longer go forward and no longer increase in wealth and power; but in most instances, in fact always, they go backward' (D, 2.2; CW, p. 329). Machiavelli further contends that the failure of princes to achieve victory in military endeavors (and thus to build empires) stems from their relative inflexibility in their capacity to adjust to new circumstances, which is required for the exercise of effective military strategy. Republics, because they are able to call upon diverse leaders at different times, overcome the limitations inherent in government by a single leader with a fixed character.

The *Discourses* are organized into three books, each of which contributes a unique line of argument in support of the overall proposition Machiavelli sets out to defend. Book 1, which at sixty chapters is the longest of the *Discourses*, examines the fundamental characteristics of republics, especially in comparison with princely regimes. Machiavelli draws heavily on historical example, rather than the more traditional tools of political philosophy, in order to demonstrate how republics are free of many of the pitfalls and shortcomings that plague the rule of a single man. Book 2 analyzes the reasons that republics, and especially Rome, have succeeded over time in the acquisition of territorial empires. Machiavelli places emphasis here on the unique capacity of republican governments to bind citizens together in order to promote common goals worthy of personal sacrifice. Finally, Book 3 addresses the dangers that confront established republican empires due to forms of corruption and decay, with special attention devoted to the ways in which self-governing cities can renew themselves and maintain control over their possessions. Responsibility for sustaining republican institutions in the context of an empire falls, in particular, on the qualities of its civil and military leaders, in conjunction with the regular reinvigoration of a sense of common purpose among the members of the citizen body.

While this brief summary of the *Discourses* does not entirely do justice to its arrangement, since Machiavelli jumps back and forth in his treatment of themes and often engages in extended digressions, we may see roughly how he develops a case favoring the strengths of republican government as a tool for territorial conquest and expansion and thus for the attainment of individual and collective glory. Indeed, he hints on more than one occasion that the return of a republic in Florence would mark the first step in a process through which the city could acquire its own empire on a scale comparable to Rome. Whether this project constitutes anything more than a vain fantasy on Machiavelli's part is entirely beside the point. Study of the history of the Roman Republic was adequate, in his mind, to demonstrate that self-government afforded the surest and safest (if not the sole) path to imperial success.

Later life and writings

The *Discourses* were clearly a labor of love, an encomium to the republican system that had nurtured Machiavelli. *The Prince* was an attempt to re-establish a connection with the political elites of Florence. While both works certainly circulated in manuscript form within his home city and elsewhere in Italy, neither brought Machiavelli employment or income, two things of which he was clearly in need. Thus, Machiavelli's enforced retirement led him to a range of other literary endeavors designed to draw greater attention to his talents. During the later 1510s and early 1520s, he penned a wide range of poetic and prose works, probably less for his personal amusement than in the hope of finding audiences appreciative of his talents and willing to support him in some way. Some of these were speeches and occasional pieces ghostwritten for others; some were works of rhyme or verse likely produced either on commission or in the hopes of finding patronage. Although a large body of these writings has survived, a more precise dating of them, and hence accurate understanding of their circumstances of composition, remains a highly speculative enterprise.

By contrast, we are on surer footing with Machiavelli's third major prose work of the 1510s. Starting perhaps soon after completion of the *Discourses*, he penned a study of *The Art of War* (published in 1521, one of his few writings printed during his lifetime), which systematizes the fundamentals of combat that he learned during his service to the Florentine republic. Dedicated to Lorenzo Strozzi, another participant in the discussions that took place at the Orti Oricellari, *The Art of War* begins with a familiar dilemma: whether a civilian population can prove able to submit itself to the rigors and sacrifices required of a well-disciplined fighting force. For Machiavelli, the life-long proponent of militias, the answer is resoundingly affirmative. Couched as a dialogue between Cosimo Rucellai, the spearhead of the Orti Oricellari group, and Fabrizio Colonna, an experienced man of arms, Machiavelli examines over the course of the seven books of *The Art of War* the qualities and training necessary for citizen soliders as well as the full range of techniques and strategies that might be deployed in order to ensure victory in combat.

Notably, Machiavelli analyzes carefully the situation of the field commander, describing his qualities with reference to the term *virtù* that he previously applied to both princes and republics as the characteristic indispensable for acquiring and maintaining control over conquered territories. A successful general, like a successful prince or city, must know how to adjust his strategies to the on-the-ground conditions that he encounters. Disaster awaits any commander who insists upon following a pre-set battle plan without regard to the terrain, to the material and human circumstances of his own forces, and to the strengths and weaknesses of the enemy. Machiavelli supplements his advice with detailed battle plans, drawn from his own experience, and observations derived both from historical example and current practices. *The Art of War* is no work of abstract theory, but a practical guide to tactics and maneuvers available to talented commanders to achieve the upper hand in battle. In the book's closing lines, Machiavelli calls it a bequest to the next generation of Florentines, who, he hopes, will put its counsel to good use in order to obtain glory for themselves and their city.

Around the same time that he was finishing the *Discourses* and composing *The Art of War*, Machiavelli also began to work in a genre new to his talents, the theatre. Initially, he adapted a work by the Roman comic author Terrence, *Woman of Andros*, and then he wrote a stage comedy entitled *The Mandrake*, both completed before 1520 (*The Mandrake* was also printed in 1521). In later 1524, he penned another comedic play, *Clizia*. Machiavelli was well suited to theatrical composition; his comedies proved popular as satires of seduction and deception, illustrating perhaps more graphically than *The Prince* or his other prose works the foibles of human nature. We do not know precisely why Machiavelli turned to the stage, but it was to bring him acclaim as well as income. *The Mandrake*, especially, remains well regarded by modern critics of Italian theatre, and productions of it continue to be staged in the present day.

The plots of Machiavelli's comedies cover ground that was well trodden by him in earlier times. *The Mandrake*, for instance, tells the story of Callimaco, a Florentine who had lived for twenty years in self-imposed exile in France but who was induced to return to his native city on the report of the presence there of a beautiful young woman, Lucrezia, married to an old and silly lawyer, Nicia. Determined to seduce Lucrezia, Callimaco arranges with his friend Ligurio to contrive an elaborate plot, with the full knowledge of Nicia, to bed her. Nicia desperately desires to have an heir, yet Lucrezia has been unable to conceive. Pretending to be a noted physician, Callimaco proposes what he claims to be a proven cure for Lucrezia's sterility: she must sleep with someone after ingesting a potion containing the root of the mandrake plant; she will become pregnant, but the man who impregnates her will die within eight days. Although initially reticent, Nicia eventually agrees and they conspire to enlist Lucrezia's mother, Sostrata, and her confessor, Friar Timoteo, to aid in the deception. While Lucrezia is at first equally hesitant to accept this plan, she, too, ultimately agrees that Nicia's relentless desire for an heir is a greater good that trumps conventional sexual morality. A series of costumed disguises leads to a confusion of identities and, in the end, to the success of Callimaco's ruse. Not only does the seduction transpire, but Callimaco reveals the entire scam to Lucrezia, who agrees to take him as her lover in perpetuity and grants him open access to her home, even convincing her husband to befriend her new paramour. Considering the situation, Lucrezia declares this outcome to be 'Heaven's wish that it be ordered so, and I am not so strong as to refuse what Heaven wills me to accept' (CW, p. 819). When produced in 1520, *The Mandrake* was instantly praised by important Florentines and was soon restaged on a number of occasions both in Machiavelli's home city and elsewhere in Italy.

Machiavelli's other major comedy, *Clizia*, seems to have been written not merely for financial gain, but also as a favor to the actress Barbara Raffacani, with whom he had become romantically entangled in the mid 1520s. Barbara was thirty years Machiavelli's junior and already a rising theatrical star, as well as a poet and a singer. Machiavelli met her at the home of a mutual acquaintance in February 1524 and was immediately smitten with her (as were many other Florentine men – she was apparently generous with her gifts). It is not difficult to see in the plot of *Clizia* direct echoes of Machiavelli's personal situation: it revolves around an old man (Nicomaco, an interesting choice of character name that seems to contain echoes of Niccolò's own name) who is inflamed with passion for a much younger woman. Again, the story develops familiar themes of duplicity, confused identities, and sexual humor and innuendo. The title character is an apparent orphan of foreign extraction and unknown lineage who has been abandoned by her kin to be raised in the home of Nicomaco and his wife, Sofronia. Clizia, a virginal seventeen-year-old, is the object of ardor not only for her adoptive father, but also for his son, Cleander. Nicomaco forbids his son from marrying his beloved, on the ostensive grounds that her family background is entirely unknown. Instead, he proposes to betroth her to his own servant, Pirro, who has promised (for a price) to share her favors with his master. In order to forestall this event, Sofronia encourages Eustachio, the steward of the family farm, to pursue Clizia as an alternative suitor, conspiring with Cleander to block Nicomaco's plan. Temporarily foiled, Nicomaco pursues various avenues (including consultation with the Church, in the person of Friar Timoteo) before hitting on the plan of a lottery to break the logjam. Pirro wins the prize, whereupon Nicomaco instructs him that, immediately after the wedding, he is to take Clizia to the house of a friend, Damon, where the master will himself deflower the maiden. But another family retainer, Siro, switches clothes with Clizia and Nicomaco winds up sleeping with the (male) servant instead, to the mirth of the entire household. In the morning, realizing that he has been tricked and shamed, Nicomaco concedes his authority over Clizia to his wife, who arranges for the marriage to Pirro to be annulled. The fate of Clizia remains an open question, until Damon arrives to report that her father – a wealthy nobleman – has come to town in search of his daughter and has been persuaded to permit her to marry Cleander. The play ends with the promise of a happy wedding, which, Sofronia says, 'will be female, and not male, like Nicomaco's' (C, 5.7; CW, p. 864). *Clizia* was first performed in early 1525 and it was, from the outset, a stunning success. The play was also Machiavelli's last foray into the theatre.

What deflected Machiavelli's attention from a potentially lucrative second career as a playwright was the revival during the 1520s of his political fortunes. Since the debacle of 1512 and its aftermath, Machiavelli had pleaded ceaselessly in his letters to his friends to assist him in finding political employment in Florence or elsewhere, requests to which for a long time they had difficulty acceding. With the death of Lorenzo de'Medici in 1519, this situation changed. Through the intervention of his well-connected friends from the Orti Oricellari discussion group

mentioned earlier, Machiavelli began to achieve some favor
with the Medici family, starting with an introduction during
March 1520 to Cardinal Giulio de'Medici, whom he apparently
impressed (not least because the Cardinal had witnessed and
been amused by a production of *The Mandrake*). Machiavelli was
soon given small assignments by the Florentine city government,
at the Cardinal's direction. In July 1520, he traveled to Lucca to
engage in minor negotiations on behalf of the city's interests; in
May 1521, he was sent to Carpi to represent Florence at a
general meeting of the Franciscan Order (during which trip he
became well acquainted with Francesco Guicciardini, then
governor of Modena and later an important Florentine official).
Cardinal de'Medici also asked Machiavelli to produce an
opinion about the question of how Florence should be governed
in the aftermath of Lorenzo's demise – a topic of considerable
debate and consternation in the city at the time. In response,
Machiavelli composed 'A Discourse on Florentine Affairs after
the Death of Lorenzo', which argues that Florence would be
best served by a well-ordered and broadly based republican
regime and that such a popular government would best serve the
interests of the Medici family. Machiavelli's espousal of a republican solution (also proposed by others in Florence) evidently did
not overly disturb the Cardinal, perhaps given the attention in
the 'Discourse' to the importance of maintaining Medici
hegemony over Florence.

Machiavelli, then, must have proved himself a sufficiently
loyal and effective agent of Florentine (and Medician) interests,
as later in 1520 he was commissioned by Cardinal de'Medici to
compose a *History of Florence*, an assignment that afforded him
the opportunity to combine for a change his political and his
literary skills in a manner that also generated much-needed
income. The scope of the commission itself was a great honor,
since it implicitly placed Machiavelli in the lineage of many of
the great Florentine humanists of the fifteenth century who had

written similar, and widely acclaimed, works. The *History of Florence* was to be Machiavelli's final major prose composition. Although the *History* has been mined for evidence of some subversive or anti-Medici tendencies, it seems to reflect the 'honest and faithful' character that Machiavelli ascribed to himself in the letter of 10 December 1513 to Vettori (MF, p. 265). Machiavelli took great care to complete this task without giving affront to the Medici clan, who were likely to view it as a litmus test of his reliability.

Yet the *History* can hardly be described as a dull chronicle of names, dates, and deeds. Indeed, Machiavelli works into its narrative many of the elements characteristic of his previous thought. Covering the period from the (mythical) earliest years of Florence until the death of the first Lorenzo de'Medici (Il Magnifico) in 1492, the eight books of the *History* concentrated on the 'glory days' of Medici ascendancy in the fifteenth century. The work is not (and does not pretend to be) a 'universal history', in the sense of recounting a set of causal mechanisms that lay behind the events he reports. Machiavelli does see factional strife as the main force driving the tumultuous times – particularly, the changes of constitutional regime and leadership – that Florence experienced. But he tends to ascribe the reasons for this conflict to the personal characteristics of the men who happened to be in positions of power at different moments in the city's history. (A model for his method can be found in his brief 'Life of Castruccio Castracani', composed in 1520.) His character sketches are not always flattering, although he seems to have softened some of them (particularly those of members of the Medici dynasty) as he worked through the process of drafting the *History*, striving to avoid giving too great offense to its patron. The book should not be afforded too great credence for its historical accuracy. Machiavelli certainly fictionalized important elements of the lives he reports, and he resorted to the technique of placing in the mouths of his 'characters' speeches that were completely his own creation. As an example of the principles of Renaissance humanist historiography, it was not especially successful. As a reflection of the dynamics of history that Machiavelli had observed through his political and intellectual career – the clash of personalities and parties – the *History* affords quite a clear illustration of its author's attitudes towards the lessons of history for politics.

The *History* is not only Machiavelli's longest extant work, but it took him more than four years to complete and polish. No doubt he wished to take great care in providing a book that would please its patron and cement his political rehabilitation, and he was also still occupied with his theatrical endeavors, his sultry affair with Barbara, his barely productive farm, and other small political assignments given to him by the city. When it was finished in 1525, Machiavelli traveled to Rome to present the *History* to the Cardinal de'Medici, who had since ascended the papal throne as Clement VII. The pope was sufficiently pleased with the result, it appears, to reward Machiavelli with a sort of 'completion bonus' for his efforts. Thereafter, other small duties were forthcoming from the Florentine government, with the apparent assent of the Medici family. If not the full rehabilitation that might have been signaled by his formal appointment to an official position, Machiavelli had achieved a large measure of his goal of returning to the good graces of the Medici.

During the years in which Machiavelli had been engaged in composing the *History* and in pursuing his other literary (and personal) interests, Italy had yet again been plunged into politically and militarily tumultuous times. The French king, Francis I, had managed to recapture Milan in 1524, but was defeated and taken prisoner by Spain the following year and forced to renounce claims to Italian territory. Upon his release from captivity, Francis immediately created an alliance with the pope and several of the major Italian powers, Florence included. This chain of events had several consequences. First, Florence itself was under imminent threat of attack and invasion by Spanish and German troops (the same forces under Emperor Charles V were to sack Rome in 1527). Moreover, the Medici, who were behind the Florentine alliance with France, had become massively unpopular in Florence, to the point where wide-scale riots broke out. Machiavelli followed the news and rumors closely, but he could have little impact on the course of events. He did advise Guicciardini and other leading magistrates in Florence's administration, but his counsel, while taken seriously, does not seem to have been put into effect.

In an ironic twist, the final days of Machiavelli's life saw both his greatest hopes realized and his greatest desires dashed. Following the entrance of the imperial troops into Rome in May 1527, Florence again freed itself from Medici control, with the citizenry joyously proclaiming a republic on 16 May. As a man of strong and longstanding republican sympathies, Machiavelli rejoiced as well, not least in the hope that he might be rewarded with his old position back, a wish kindled by some of his friends. Ultimately, his former post as Second Chancellor was awarded to another man, for reasons about which we can only speculate: perhaps his recent work on behalf of the Medici led some to suspect his loyalties; maybe his lurid reputation, generated both by his personal conduct and by his literary output, placed him beyond the pale; or perhaps his relative seniority disqualified him – an act of age discrimination. Whatever the reason or combination of reasons, the restored Florentine republic that he had advocated for so long rebuffed him. This final disappointment heralded his demise. Almost immediately after the word came in mid June that the office of the Second Chancellor had been filled by someone else, Machiavelli fell seriously ill. He died on 21 June 1527 and was buried the following day in the church of Santa Croce in Florence.

2
Heavens/earth

Despite his wide reputation as irreverent, impious and irreligious – if not downright atheistic – Machiavelli was noticeably concerned by the effects that supernatural forces exercised on humankind. There is virtually no part of Machiavelli's corpus that does not include reference to the heavenly realms, often described in terms of the power of *Fortuna*, the goddess of earthly change. As he states in the *Discourses*, 'If we observe carefully how human affairs go on, many times we see that things come up and events take place against which the Heavens do not wish any provision to be made ... Men are able to assist Fortune, but not to thwart her. They can weave her designs but cannot destroy them' (D, 2.29; CW, pp. 406, 408). Recognition of the impact of celestial forces is echoed elsewhere in the *Discourses*: 'To achieve something good is difficult unless Fortune, aiding you, with her power overcomes' the obstacles set for human beings (D, 3.37; CW, p. 512). *The Prince* is rife with similar remarks. From the dedicatory epistle onwards, fortune is cited as the cause of the 'greatness' or the 'malice' that people experience (P, Dedication; CW, p. 11). Machiavelli concludes the famous chapter 25 of *The Prince* ('Fortune's Power in Human Affairs and How She Can Be Forestalled') with the declaration that 'men are successful when they are in close harmony with Fortune, and when they are out of harmony, they are unsuccessful' (P, 25; CW, p. 92). Human beings are victims of fortune; and fortune itself is aligned with heavenly motions and forces. Any ruler who counts on fortune to support him, or who bases his decisions and policies on the previous course of events, will inevitably be disappointed and eventually destroyed.

The supernatural

Tempting as it may be to view Machiavelli's obsession with fortune as a function of his own political troubles with the Medici during the 1510s, he in fact devoted considerable attention to the sway of supernatural power long before he composed *The Prince* and the *Discourses*. In a 1506 letter commonly known as the *Ghiribizzi* (meaning 'Fantasies' or 'Speculations'), addressed to Piero Soderini's nephew, Giovan Battista Soderini, Machiavelli already expressed preoccupation with how the fluctuations of fortune dominate sublunar (that is, earthly) events. The basic quandary, he observes, stems from the sheer unpredictability of political success or failure. On the one hand, different routes to the same goal may prove equally effective; there is no single universal set of rules that assures the outcomes that one desires. On the other hand, Machiavelli notes that calculation and deliberation often lead to ruin; the best-laid plans regularly do not hit their mark. 'Sometimes the way of doing things that was praised when it led to conquest is vilified when it leads to defeat, and sometimes when defeat comes after long prosperity ... people do not blame anything of their own but rather indict heaven and the will of the Fates. But the reason why different actions are sometimes useful and sometimes equally detrimental I do not know – yet I should very much like to' (MF, p. 135). In sum, foresight – the ability to understand the pattern of earthly events in order to ensure that one consistently attains the results one seeks – seems entirely beyond human grasp.

Despite his self-professed ignorance about the proper explanation for this predicament, Machiavelli proposes to offer his own account in order, he says, to elicit his correspondent's (unrecorded) response. He posits a fundamental uniformity of human character: 'Just as Nature has created men with different faces, so she has created them with different intellects and imaginations. As a result, each man behaves according to his own intellect and imagination' (MF, p.135). In sum, people each have special traits or qualities that are fixed and unchanging (a topic that will be explored in greater detail in chapter 3), such that they act wholly on the basis of their individual properties consistently and predictably. This natural permanence of character can lead to markedly different consequences. The person whose particular abilities 'suit the times', in the sense that they match what the circumstances call for, will succeed so long as the situation remains stable. When piety proves useful to maintaining authority, the pious man will be ascendant; when cruelty is needed, a cruel character will achieve great things. So long as the conditions remain fundamentally steady and predictable, the continued success of a person possessing the requisite character will be assured. The problem, however, is that times change and men do not and cannot change with them. This seems to be fundamentally what Machiavelli regards to be the effect of fortune: the incongruity between how people act and what circumstances demand:

> The man who matches his way of doing things with the conditions of the times is successful; the man whose actions are at odds with the times and the pattern of events is unsuccessful. Hence it can be that two men can achieve the same goal by acting differently: because each one of them matches his actions to what he encounters and because there are as many patterns of events as there are regions and governments. But because times and affairs often change – both in general and in particular – and because men change neither their imaginations nor their ways of doing things accordingly, it turns out that a man has good fortune at one time and bad fortune at another ... thus it follows that Fortune is fickle, controlling men and keeping them under her yoke.

> (MF, p. 135)

Humanity appears trapped by a kind of metaphysical dilemma: our characters are naturally uniform, but changing circumstances call for variation in response to the times. Viewed from the perspective of earthly human existence, there is no apparent way to guarantee that one can always overcome fortune. At best, Machiavelli suggests that to adopt the boldness of youth and to refrain from following consistent patterns of behavior – in sum, to imitate the very fickleness of fortune – might produce some good result (MF, p. 134). But the success of such a strategy cannot be predicted with any reliability. The conclusion to be drawn from Machiavelli's speculations is an essentially negative and pessimistic one.

This bleak impression is reinforced when we turn to another of Machiavelli's early writings, the poetic 'Tercets on Fortune', which was also dedicated to Giovan Battista Soderini and may have been composed at about the same time as the *Ghiribizzi*. *Fortuna* is fully personified in the 'Tercets', as in Machiavelli's more famous writings: she is an 'unstable goddess and fickle deity' who 'times events as suits her; she raises us up, she puts us down without pity, without law or right' (CW, p. 746). Machiavelli lists all of the great kingdoms and empires that have been made and unmade by *Fortuna*, and he laments her dominance even over men who possessed exceptional natural endowments. Neither individuals nor societies are exempt from submission to fortune: 'Not a thing in the world is eternal; Fortune wills it so and makes herself splendid by it, so that her power may be more clearly seen' (CW, p. 748). Of course, Machiavelli avers, men do themselves no good by ascribing to her only the bad that happens to them, when in fact she is the source of good as well as evil events. *Fortuna* is 'omnipotent' (CW, p. 745) and the many wheels contained in her heavenly palace spin out riches, health, and power as well as poverty, illness, and servitude. The ability of fortune to achieve these effects is traced, as in the *Ghiribizzi*, to the congruity or incongruity between personality and the whims of the goddess:

> That man most luckily forms his plan, among all the persons in
>   Fortune's palace, who chooses a wheel befitting her wish,
> since the inclinations that make you act, so far as they conform
>   with her doings, are the causes of your good and your ill.
> Yet you cannot therefore trust yourself to her nor hope to
>   escape her hard bite, her hard blows, violent and cruel,
> because while you are whirled about by the rim of a wheel that
>   for the moment is lucky and good, she is wont to reverse its
>   course in midcircle.

(CW, p. 747)

Machiavelli implies that one ought to despair finding some single tactic for conquering *Fortuna* and inducing her always to accede to one's wishes; her fickle ways are too inscrutable for mortal men to discern. Enmeshed in the constancy of our own personal traits, we cannot vary our behavior as the times require. Although Machiavelli once again hints that 'audacity' and 'youth' might receive special favor for a while, it is still too easy to grow complacent and age takes its toll (CW, p. 746). The grim conclusion that fortune is too powerful a force for anyone to overcome is sustained in the 'Tercets on Fortune'.

Thus, the dominance of supernatural forces (there is consistent equation of *Fortuna* with 'Heaven' or 'the heavens') over human life deeply troubled Machiavelli even before the downturn of his own fortune. The issue is taken up again by him time and again throughout his later life, perhaps most notably in chapter 25 of *The Prince*. *Fortuna* is portrayed there as analogous to a raging river: 'She shows her power where strength and wisdom do not prepare to resist her, and directs her fury where she knows that no dykes and embankments are ready to hold her' (P, 25; CW, p. 90). (Machiavelli speaks from some experience here; recall his enterprise in collaboration with Leonardo da Vinci to redirect the flow of the river around Pisa.) Machiavelli restates the same basic dilemmas that he posed in the *Ghiribizzi*. How do the same human qualities lead to different outcomes and opposite traits produce the same result? Why do successful rulers suddenly and without any change in policy fail? Likewise, his terms of analysis remain largely the same in *The Prince* as in his previous writings:

> In the things that lead them to the end they seek, that is, glory and riches, men act in different ways: one with caution, another impetuously; one by force, the other with skill; one by patience, the other with its contrary; and all of them with these differing methods attain their ends. We find also that of two cautious men, one carries out his purpose, the other does not. Likewise, we find two men with differing temperaments equally successful, one being cautious and the other impetuous. This results from nothing else than the nature of the times, which is harmonious or not with their procedure. From that results what I have said: that two men, working differently, secure the same outcome; and of two working in the same way, one attains his end, and the other does not. On this depends variations in success: if, for one whose policy is caution and patience, times and affairs circle about in such a way that his policy is good, he continues to succeed; if times and affairs change, he falls, because he does not change his way of proceeding.
>
> (P, 25; CW, p. 91)

The congruity between the circling wheels of fortune and the characteristics of specific men ensures success, albeit of a temporary sort; but when circumstances change, the successful are ruined and new qualities are called for.

Machiavelli illustrates this view with reference to the career of Pope Julius II, who was favored by *Fortuna*. Impetuous by nature, Julius attained his goals solely on account of the fact that 'the times and their circumstances [were] so in harmony with his own way of proceeding that he was always successful' (P, 25; CW, p. 91). Of course, Julius was saved from the negative effects of fortune by his premature death, 'because if times had come when he needed to proceed with caution, they would have brought about his downfall; for never would he have turned away from those methods to which his nature inclined him' (P, 25; CW, p. 92). Still, Machiavelli contends, such impetuousness is generally to be preferred as a strategy should one have no inkling of the conditions that *Fortuna* has laid down. In a somewhat infamous comparison, he points out that *Fortuna*, being a woman, is better vanquished by force than by cold calculation: 'Like a woman, she is the friend of young men, because they are less cautious, more spirited, and with more boldness master her' (P, 25; CW, p. 92). To be sure, Machiavelli does not regard such youthful aggressiveness as any insurance of permanent conquest of fortune. His major, and overarching, observation about the preponderant power of fortune over earthly human life stands: 'I conclude then (with Fortune varying and men remaining stubborn in their ways) that men are successful when they are in close harmony with Fortune and when they are out of harmony they are unsuccessful' (P, 25; CW, p. 92). It seems, in short, that the prospects for sustained good fortune are non-existent, given the fixed properties of human nature that resist variation with circumstance.

Cosmological principles

Machiavelli's evident pessimism clearly depends upon an overarching conception of the role played by forces outside of human control – the supernatural power enjoyed by *Fortuna* and 'the heavens' – in dictating the circumstances in which human beings are compelled to act. In short, his thought has a pronounced cosmological dimension. We are offered a glimpse into the cluster of concepts and terminology associated with Machiavelli's cosmology in a passage of 'The Ass', worth quoting at length, in which the sources of human misfortune are explained:

> But because weeping has always been shameful to a man, he should turn to the blows of Fortune a face unstained with tears.
>
> You see the stars and the sky, you see the moon, you see the other planets go wandering, now high, now low, without any rest;
>
> sometimes you see the sky cloudy, sometimes shining and clear, and likewise nothing on earth remains in the same condition always.
>
> From this result peace and war; on this depends the hatreds among those whom one wall and one moat shut up together.
>
> From this came your first suffering; this was altogether the cause of your toils without reward.
>
> Not yet has Heaven altered its opinion, nor will alter it, while the Fates keep toward you their hard purpose.
>
> And those feelings which you have found so hostile and so adverse are not yet, not yet purged;
>
> but when their roots are dry, and the Heavens show themselves gracious, times happier than ever before will return;
>
> and so pleasant and delightful they will be that you will get joy from the memory of both past and future affliction.
>
> Perhaps you will yet take pride in retelling to various people the long account of your sufferings.
>
> But before the stars show themselves propitious toward you, you will have to travel to explore the world …

because that Providence which supports the human species
intends you to bear this affliction for your greater good ...
There can be no change in this harsh star; by putting you in this
place, the ill is deferred, not canceled.

(CW, pp. 757–8)

The ferocity of the Machiavellian cosmology has sometimes left
the impression that his worldview is essentially non-Christian,
since he appears to view the universe as fundamentally hostile to
human aims, rather than as the creation of a benevolent God.
Although many previous Christian thinkers had also employed
the theme of fortune in their writings, they tended to use it as
an equivalent for Providence or a similar divine power that,
while inscrutable to non-believers, could be accessed by
members of the faithful. Consequently, Machiavelli quite often
stands accused of adopting a pagan or pre-Christian conception
of supernatural forces.

Should this judgment about Machiavelli's cosmological
worldview be sustained? To be sure, Machiavelli was no
friend of the institutionalized Christian Church as he knew it.
The *Discourses* makes clear that conventional Christianity saps
from human beings the vigor required for active public life.
Christianity, he declares, 'makes us esteem less the honor of
the world' and thus glorifies 'humble and contemplative men
rather than active ones'. Consequently, Christian religion
promotes 'sloth' rather than the 'vigor' necessary for the
performance of patriotic duties (D, 2.2; CW, p. 331). In a
similar vein, *The Prince* speaks with equal parts disdain and
admiration about the current condition of the Church and its
Pope (P, 11; CW, pp. 44–6). Such passages have been taken as
evidence that Machiavelli was himself profoundly anti-
Christian, preferring the pagan civil religions of ancient
societies such as Rome, which he regarded as more suitable for
a city endowed with *virtù*. At best, Machiavelli has been

described as a man of conventional, if unenthusiastic, piety, prepared to bow to the externalities of worship but not deeply devoted in either soul or mind to the tenets of Christian faith.

Machiavelli's attitude toward religion and the supernatural realm in general is, however, more complex than has usually been credited. His views on 'the heavens' and their relation to the earth might be better described as a sort of reconstitution and reinvigoration of Christian doctrines by supplementing them with the political virtues of Roman civil religion in order to promote a conception of humankind as capable of actions that permit the overcoming of fortune. In sum, he advocated a 'politicized' version of Christianity suitable for an active civil life. He did not hold to the humanistic assumption that individuals are entirely capable of making their own choices and guiding their own conduct apart from occult forces. Rather, Machiavelli believed in human cooperation with the supernatural plan by seeking to discover its meaning and discern how it could be employed to achieve earthly success. This is apparent, for instance, from his repeated assertions that one element of political achievement, and hence the conquest of fortune, stems from grasping stellar (and hence divine) principles. The *Discourses* affords a clear example of this position: 'What causes it I do not know, but both ancient and modern instances indicate that nothing important ever happens in a city or a region that has not been foretold either by diviners or by revelations or by prodigies or by other celestial signs' (D, 1.56; CW, p. 311). Machiavelli points to Savonarola's prediction of the 1494 French invasion of Italy, as well as portents widely observed in Tuscany; he mentions the strange lightning strikes that immediately preceded the death of Lorenzo d'Medici Il Magnifico and the downfall of his own master, Piero Soderini. Machiavelli speculates that the key to political opportunity is held by those who are qualified to interpret correctly such events whose meanings are otherwise hidden, and he explicitly invokes the cosmological beliefs held by Christianity:

> The cause of this I believe should be considered and interpreted by a man who has knowledge of things natural and supernatural, which we do not have. Yet it could be that since, as some philosophers hold, the air about us is full of intelligences – and these through their natural abilities foreseeing future things and having compassion on men – these spirits warn men with such signs, so they can prepare for resistance. At any rate, however it is, so the truth seems to be; and always after such strange events new things happen to countries.
>
> (D, 1.56; CW, pp. 311–12).

Machiavelli seems to embrace a cosmological principle that opens up the possibility of foreknowing future events by supernatural means. He teaches the lesson here that those who enjoy occult knowledge are not restrained by the limits otherwise imposed by fortune. Indeed, they may achieve immunity from misfortune and full control over themselves.

Consequently, despite his apparent pessimism in writings such as the *Ghiribizzi*, the 'Tercets on Fortune', and *The Prince*, Machiavelli ultimately rejects a conception of fortune as a wholly autonomous (and largely malevolent, or at least indifferent) force in human life. He consistently implies instead that there is some plan (however inscrutable) standing behind the course of human events. This is evident in his remarks that fortune or the heavens or some other occult power actively selects certain individuals for a special role in history. Speaking in the *Discourses* of the reform of a corrupt city, he states,

> Truly the heavens cannot give a greater opportunity for glory ... Those to whom the Heavens give such an occasion should observe the two roads put before them: one makes their lives

secure and after death renders them famous; the other makes them live in continual anxieties and after death leaves them an ill repute that never ends.

(D, 1.10; CW, p. 223)

From this, one may conclude that individuals are selected by a power or force outside of themselves for the task of leadership (although they still utilize their free choice in taking advantage of their opportunities, as we shall see). The active quality of supernatural design is also emphasized elsewhere in the *Discourses*:

Men who commonly live amid great troubles or great successes deserve less praise or blame, because most of the time we see that they have been pushed into a destructive or elevated action by some great advantage that the Heavens have bestowed on them, giving them the opportunity – or taking it away from them – to work effectively. Skillfully Fortune does this, since she chooses a man, when she plans to bring about great things, who is of so much perception and so much ability that he recognizes the opportunities she puts before him.

(D, 2.29; CW, p. 407)

Likewise, in *The Prince*, the capacity of the ruler to 'recognize the ills in his state when they spring up … is given to a very few' (P, 13; CW, p. 54). That some plan or wisdom stands behind fortune forms an article of faith in Machiavelli's thought. Even if the scheme cannot be discerned by most people (hence, the arbitrary appearance of fortune to most men at most times), it is present. Indeed, this counts for Machiavelli as a reason for optimism: people 'ought never to give up as beaten, because, since they do not know [Fortune's] purpose, and since she goes through crooked and unknown roads, they can always hope' (D, 2.29; CW, p. 408). To make the observation that fortune is purposive, even providential, is already to dispel as a by-product of human ignorance the notion that events and circumstances are without rhyme or reason.

Overcoming fortune

Machiavelli's conception of the relationship between fortune and a wider supernatural scheme does not, however, render human beings the powerless playthings of some great divinely ordained design. In *The Prince*, he repeatedly defends the view that the only truly safe means of acquiring a state is through the exercise of one's abilities, rather than by means of fortune, since rulers who depend upon chance circumstance to maintain themselves are invariably frustrated in achieving their goal. 'He who depends least on Fortune sustains himself longest', Machiavelli asserts, 'Those who ... become princes simply through Fortune may become so with little effort, but with much effort sustain themselves' (P, 7; CW, p. 27). Yet at the same time, he realizes that fortune is the source of all opportunities to govern; no one can achieve rulership if he is opposed by fortune. But the examples of princes held in highest esteem by Machiavelli are drawn from among those who 'had from Fortune nothing more than opportunity, which gave them matter into which they could introduce whatever form they chose; and without opportunity, their strength of will would have been wasted, and without such strength the opportunity would have been useless' (P, 6; CW, p. 25). This, then, seems to form the essence of achieving political success: knowing when one is well situated to act and grasping the opportunity. The character Fabrizio (who speaks with Machiavelli's voice) in *The Art of War*, reflecting on what he might have achieved, underscores the idea of cooperating with circumstance in implementing one's plans. 'Yet assuredly if Fortune had in the past granted me a state large enough to permit such an attempt to put the proper principles of organizing an army and conducting war into effect,' Fabrizio laments, 'I believe that in a short time I could have shown the world how much ancient customs are worth. Without doubt, I would have made my state greater or lost it without shame' (AW, 7; CW, p. 726). The heavens determine one's opportunities, but one's learning and insight afford one the ability to put one's chances to the best use.

Consequently, the skills, talents, and abilities that the successful ruler needs cannot be activated without some supernatural element. Consider Machiavelli's declaration in one of his works of poetry, the 'Second Decennale':

> Oh proud men, ever you have arrogant faces, you who hold the
> > scepters and the crowns, and of the future you do not know
> > a single truth!
> So blinded are you by your present greed which over your eyes
> > holds a thick veil that things remote you cannot see.
> From this it comes that heaven, shifting from this to that, shifts
> > your states more often than the heat and the ice are
> > changed, because if you turned your prudence to learning
> > the ill and finding its remedy, such great power from
> > heaven would be taken.

> (CW, p. 1461)

Rulers must set aside mundane interests and come to understand how the celestial realm guides sublunar events. Once they do so, they will be able to gain the foresight they require in order to escape from the throes of fortune. The role of a political advisor such as Machiavelli is thus at best only preparatory, as he himself admits in the Preface to the second book of the *Discourses*: 'It is the duty of the good man to teach others anything of value that through the malice of the times and of Fortune you have been unable to put into effect, in order that since many will know of it, some of them more loved by Heaven may be ready to put it into effect' (D, 3.Preface; CW, p. 324). To the extent that the individual is the source of his own success, Machiavelli supposes, this is a function of one's attuned and educated insight and intellect cooperating with a divinely ordered scheme. Thus, Machiavelli's solution to the predicament with which he was obsessed – the inability of human beings to conquer fortune permanently – drew directly upon central tenets of Christian belief. Transcendence of mere earthly affairs and grasping their supernatural significance constitute the sole source of control over temporal events.

Thus, completely fatalistic resignation is not in keeping with Machiavelli's teachings. While certainly attracted to a deterministic stance in order to explain both the failure and the success of human initiative in overcoming events, he does not utterly surrender human efficacy. This is suggested, for example, by the opening paragraph of chapter 25 of *The Prince*:

> I am not unaware that many have thought, and still think, that the affairs of the world are so ruled by fortune and by God that human prudence is incapable of controlling them, as a result of which nothing that goes astray has a remedy; and therefore it could be judged that it is useless to worry too much about things, but let them be governed by happenstance … When I think about this, I am sometimes inclined, to some extent, to share this opinion. Nevertheless, so as not to eliminate our free will (*libero arbitrio*), I judge it to be the case that fortune is the arbiter of half our actions, but that it lets us control roughly the other half.

> (P, 25; CW, pp. 89–90)

The way in which Machiavelli has phrased his observation is revealing, in particular because of his use of the technical Latin term for freedom of the will, *liberum arbitrium*, in a theological sense. This acknowledgement of the human capacity to will freely appears to admit that the effects of supernatural forces may be rendered compatible with the human ability to master one's fate through knowledge and action. One might, then, summarize Machiavelli's position as follows. No one ought to think that he is capable, purely by dint of his own abilities and talents, of acquiring and maintaining a state; the limitations imposed from outside by fortune, as well as intrinsic constraints of human nature and character, are too formidable. Instead, the only effective ruler is one who grasps the meanings that lay behind apparently capricious fortune and hence discerns divine purposes.

That Machiavelli had something very like this position in mind is confirmed by a remark in chapter 26 of *The Prince*, just following an account (which is discussed below) of heavenly portents of Medici success: 'Everything points to your greatness. The rest you must do yourself. God does not do everything, so as not to take from us *libero arbitrio* and part of the glory that pertains to us' (P, 26; CW, p. 94). Heavenly selection must not be an excuse for passivity, as though achievements will fall into one's lap without effort. God provides the opportunity and the means for success, but the will of the chosen individual must still be exercised, his personal talents must be displayed. As Machiavelli asserts in 'The Ass',

> To believe that without effort on your part God fights for you, while you are idle and on your knees, has ruined many kingdoms and many states.
> There is assuredly need for prayers; and altogether mad is he who forbids people their ceremonies and their devotions;
> because in fact it seems that from them may be reaped union and good order; and on them in turn rests good and happy fortune.

> But there should be no one with so small a brain that he will
>   believe, if his house is falling, that God will save it without
>   any other prop,
> because he will die beneath that ruin.

(CW, p. 764)

Machiavelli's lesson is clear: God's call to action, an awakening
of the free will, comes with the assurance that the course of
conduct undertaken will produce the redemption sought. Only
the 'redemption' in question is not personal salvation, but the
attainment of a public salvation of the citizens and subjects over
whom the ruler governs and the consequent realization of his
own glory.

God's friendship

Whence arises the special knowledge that permits men to bind
the heavens to their wills? Machiavelli takes this out of the hands
of purely human determination. Rather, those who succeed –
albeit through their own freely chosen actions – do so because
they enjoy God's grace. The theme of grace is one that runs
throughout Machiavelli's works, including such expressions of
conventional Christian piety as 'An Exhortation to Penitence'
and 'Allocution Made to a Magistrate', two short works probably composed on commission during the 1520s. In the former
work especially, a clearly Christian God is portrayed as a giver of
gifts, and in turn the greatest sin human beings can commit is to
be ungrateful to Him.

> In order to realize our ingratitude, it is necessary to consider
> how many and of what sort are the benefits we have received
> from God. Consider, then, how all things made and created are
> made and created for the benefit of man ... Consider the beauty

of the things we see. Of these, part he has made for our use,
part in order that, as we observe the glory and the marvelous
workmanship of these things, upon us may come a thirst and a
longing to possess those other things that are hidden from us ...
See, then, with how much ingratitude man rises against such a
great benefactor! And how much punishment he deserves when
he perverts the use of these things and turns them toward evil!

(CW, p. 172)

Machiavelli's God is one who has bestowed upon humankind
every favor – from material goods and resources to speech and
reason – and who thereby demands penitence from those who
do not accept and appreciate the great gifts they have been
granted. Nor is penitence understood in terms of inward contri-
tion alone; it must be manifest in actions consistent with grate-
fulness for what God has given us (CW, pp. 173–4). The
gracious nature of the Machiavellian deity thus directly correlates to the function of assigning personal destiny that is allotted
to fortune and the heavens elsewhere in his writings.

In *The Prince*, likewise, Machiavelli acknowledges the one
certain guarantee that fortune may be overcome: the gift of
grace granted by God. In chapter 6, he singles out a few men
'who through their own ability and not through Fortune have
been transformed into princes[:] ... Moses, Cyrus, Romulus,
Theseus, and the like' (P, 6; CW, p. 25). In Machiavelli's view,
Moses seems to be the greatest among these. The obvious reason
for this, as stated in the *Discourses*, is that 'among all famous men
those are most famous who have been heads and organizers of
religion. Next after them are those who have founded either
republics or kingdoms' (D, 1.10; CW, p. 220). Moses thus
stands atop Machiavelli's list of glorious men: alone among those
illustrations that he offers, Moses was the founder of both a
religion and a state. The awe in which Machiavelli holds Moses
is evident in *The Prince*. 'Although Moses should not be

discussed, since he was a mere executor for things laid down for him by God, nevertheless he ought to be exalted, if only for the grace (*grazia*) that made him worthy to speak with God' (P, 6; CW, p. 25). Moses was God's chosen, His anointed. Machiavelli notes later in the chapter – making a pointed contrast with Savonarola – that Moses was the ultimate 'armed prophet', prepared to employ force in a righteous cause against those who would oppose God's will (P, 6; CW, pp. 26–7). As Machiavelli observes in the *Discourses*, 'He who reads the Bible intelligently sees that if Moses was to put his laws and regulations into effect, he was forced to kill countless men who, moved by nothing else than envy, were opposed to his plan' (D, 3.30; CW, p. 496). Machiavelli finds in God's grace an authorization to act as necessary for the sake of realizing a divine scheme. Having been selected to receive God's favor does not constrain the range of options available to the ruler. If anything, the graced prince may act with greater impunity, knowing that his cause is righteous and that he enjoys an extraterrestrial assurance of a successful end to his endeavors.

Yet might not we say that Moses is unique in this regard, as the only prince on Machiavelli's list who actually converses with God (at least if one discounts 'unarmed prophets' such as Savonarola)? While Machiavelli clearly singles Moses out for special praise, however, he does not mean to suggest that the case of the Old Testament figure is entirely unique. Rather, he remarks, 'But look at Cyrus and the others who gained and founded kingdoms. You will find them all amazing; and if you look at their actions and their individual methods, they seem no different than those of Moses, who had so great a teacher' (P, 6; CW, p. 25). While Moses certainly benefited from direct divine guidance, the other founders whom Machiavelli praises also enjoyed some special favor from God, both in terms of the gift of an opportunity for acting propitiously and the divine encouragement to seize the chance that they had been granted. The possession of divine inspiration is the most fundamental source of the similarities between Moses, Cyrus, Romulus, and Theseus. For what other reason would Machiavelli term all new rulers – not simply Moses – 'prophets' (P, 6; CW, p. 26)?

The idea that secular rulers, no less than theocratic ones, are agents of the divine will and serve at God's pleasure is not so contrary to conventional religion as it may seem at first glance. Rather, the worthiness of the greatest pagan rulers in the eyes of God was upheld by medieval thinkers. Witness the story of the Emperor Trajan, widely recounted during the Middle Ages: so just was he that, although a pagan, he was saved from the tortures of Hell after the intervention of Pope Gregory the Great with God. Machiavelli indeed knew this tale, for in his 'Allocation Made to a Magistrate', he cites Trajan's example of justice, quoting in this connection from Dante's *Purgatorio* and concluding, 'From this we can see how much God loves Justice and mercy' (AMM, pp. 526–7). Nor is Machiavelli's description of Cyrus as an 'armed prophet' on par with Moses especially sacrilegious. Rather, to claim that the success of rulers depends upon a gift directly from God, regardless of whether they enjoy some immediate relationship with the divine being, was a hallmark of Christian thought long before *The Prince*. At best, Machiavelli is simply adapting this tradition to explain how the greatest princes have managed to overcome the limitations imposed by fortune as well as their own natures and characters: they benefited from God's aid.

In the final chapter of *The Prince*, Machiavelli returns to the theme that rulers are sure to succeed only when the hand of God assists them. His goal is to implore the Medici family to look upon themselves as the new 'redeemers' of Italy. In this regard, he compares the current predicament of Italy with the situations encountered by Moses among the Hebrews, Cyrus in Persia, and Theseus in Athens: in all cases, the nation was 'without leadership, without order, beaten, despoiled, lacerated, devastated, subject to every sort of ruination', in sum, ready for a new founding (P, 26; CW, pp. 92–3). Just as God had once granted the opportunity to act gloriously to His earlier 'armed prophets', so it exists in Machiavelli's own day. Indeed, *The Prince* in this passage overtly invokes the divine dimension of Italy's need for salvation, identifying God's hand both in the existence of propitious circumstances and in the selection of a leader:

> And though up to now various gleams have appeared in some Italians from which we might judge them ordained by God for her redemption, nevertheless we have seen that, in the highest course of their actions, they have been disapproved by Fortune … [Italy] is now praying to God to send someone to redeem her from such barbarous cruelty and arrogance … There is not, at present, anyone in whom she can have more hope than in your glorious family, which, through its fortune and its wisdom and strength, favored by God and by the Church (of which it is now head), can make itself the leader of this redemption. This will not be very hard if you bring before you the actions and lives of those named above [viz., Moses, Cyrus, and Theseus]. And although these men were exceptional and marvelous, nevertheless they were men; and every one of them had a poorer chance than the present one, because their undertaking was not more just than this, nor easier, nor was God more friendly to them than to you.
>
> (P, 26; CW, pp. 93–4)

Machiavelli then goes on to list numerous omens and portents which accord perfectly with the occultism that forms part and parcel of his Christian belief system. He proclaims that 'now we see marvelous, unexampled signs that God is directing you: the sea is divided; a cloud shows you the road; the rock pours out water; manna rains down …' (P, 26; CW, p. 94). These statements perhaps constitute the most extreme illustration of Machiavelli's reliance upon a Christian worldview that made room for the sublunar understanding of supernatural plans. From this, he concludes that human beings cannot overcome the obstacles to rulership on their own, but must be selected by divine grace, and thereby authorized by God's providence, in order to assure success.

Is the intimation of the divine appointment of the Medici mere hyperbole or even sheer flattery on Machiavelli's part? Many of his readers have certainly suspected as much. But it should be evident that Machiavelli's theologically flavored forecast is entirely consistent with his remarks about grace elsewhere in his corpus. Not only does Machiavelli articulate an internally consistent position with regard to the divine design regarding earthly political affairs, but he does so in a manner that perpetuates Christian doctrines. And his reliance upon God's ordination and grace has a very serious and important purpose: to act as a counterweight to the claim that the forces of fortune necessarily constrain the ability of people to succeed in the conduct of government.

3
Nature/innovation

In the previous chapter, we saw how Machiavelli developed a guarded assessment of the ability of human beings to achieve political success on their own terms and apart from the realization that they are subject to conditions imposed by 'the heavens'. In turn, the supernatural realm is guided by a divine plan that is difficult for most people to discern, at least without God's inspiration and 'friendship'. While not as pessimistic in its consequences as it sometimes sounds, Machiavelli's cosmology does not endorse a thorough-going humanist perspective that empowers men to attain their earthly goals entirely (or even mainly) by means of their own plans and calculations. Machiavelli's conception of human nature, especially of the psychological make-up of humankind, supports and reinforces this framework. At the same time, there seems to be another dimension to Machiavelli's thought that cuts in a different direction, namely, his idea that human beings (individually and collectively) are capable of acquiring a certain set of qualities that permit them a wide latitude in controlling their circumstances and conquering fortune for more than a short period of time. In other words, human beings are innovative creatures who invent new ways of acting and new forms of political life that resist the vicissitudes of *Fortuna*.

Human nature(s)

The word that Machiavelli employs to capture and summarize these inventive characteristics is *virtù*. While the Italian term would normally be translated into English as 'virtue' and would ordinarily convey the connotation of conventional moral goodness, Machiavelli obviously means something very different when he refers to the *virtù* of the prince. In *The Prince*, Machiavelli employs the concept of *virtù* to refer to the range of personal traits that a ruler will find it necessary to acquire in order to 'maintain his state' and to 'achieve great things', the two standard markers of power for him. This makes it clear there can be no equivalence between the conventional virtues and Machiavellian *virtù*. Machiavelli expects princes of full *virtù* to be capable, as the situation requires, of behaving in a completely evil fashion. For the circumstances of political activity are such that conduct otherwise considered to be morally vicious can never be excluded from the realm of possible actions in which the prince may have to engage. Machiavelli's sense of what it is to be a leader of *virtù* can thus be summarized by his recommendation that the prince above all else must acquire a 'flexible disposition'. That person is best suited for office, on Machiavelli's account, who is capable of varying his conduct from good to evil and back again as fortune and circumstances dictate (P, 18; CW, p. 66). The conduct that Machiavelli counsels political agents to perform may at times be inconsistent with the deeds classified as virtuous. The admissibility of cruelty, deceit, physical violence, and an array of other conventional vices into the range of acceptable human behavior demarcates Machiavelli as a very singular kind of moralist – if a moralist at all. *Virtù* denotes the ensemble of personal qualities and traits that provide the touchstone of political success.

At first glance, the idea of *virtù* fits uncomfortably with Machiavelli's doctrines of human nature and behavior. Throughout his works, Machiavelli espouses a two-pronged conception of motivation and conduct. The first part of this teaching involves a universalized set of principles, derived from his observations about why people act. Machiavelli expresses this succinctly in *The Prince*: 'we can say this about men in general: they are ungrateful, changeable, simulators and dissimulators, runaways from danger, eager for gain', in short, self-interested, wicked, and evil in the conventional sense (P, 17; CW, p. 62). This claim is often regarded to represent the quintessential Machiavellian opinion about human nature. Rulers must resort to deception, violence, treachery, and the other techniques that Machiavelli is known to advocate because they have to assume that those whom they govern are fundamentally self-seeking and unreliable. 'For there is such a difference between how men live and how they ought to live that he who abandons what is done for what ought to be done earns his destruction rather than his preservation', Machiavelli counsels, 'because any man who under all conditions insists on making it his business to be good will surely be destroyed among so many who are not good' (P, 15; CW, pp. 57–8). Nor is this theme confined to *The Prince*. Machiavelli's 'Tercets on Ambition', probably written before the end of 1509, contains a lengthy description of the human condition as an unending quest for personal advantage:

> Oh human spirit, insatiable, crafty, arrogant, and shifting, and above all else malignant, iniquitous, violent, and savage,
> because through your longing so ambitious, the first violent death was seen in the world, and the first grass red with blood!
> Since this evil seed is now mature, since evil's cause is multiplied, there is no reason for men to repent of doing evil.
>
> (CW, p. 736)

Another poem, the 'Tercets on Ingratitude', finished before 1515, echoes a similar idea of man's fundamentally self-regarding nature (CW, pp. 740–4). Likewise, the *Discourses* counsels that the design of a well-ordered republic must 'presuppose that all men are evil and that they are always going to act according to the wickedness of their spirits whenever they have free scope' (D, 1.3; CW, p. 201). Human beings, in Machiavelli's view, then, can usually be counted on to look after themselves and their immediate advantage (most concretely, property and family) and to eschew actions that require sacrifice for the good of others. Moreover, this extends to group interests. In principalities and even in republics, the nobility and the masses have different and conflicting aims that fundamentally direct their actions, often (although not necessarily) with disastrous consequences, a topic to which we shall return in later chapters.

In addition to this broad conception of the construction of human psychology, Machiavelli posits the existence of fixed individual human character, endowed by nature or the heavens, which was discussed in chapter 2. He upholds the position that human action arises out of a set of personal characteristics that are firmly rooted and relatively insusceptible to variation or erasure. Thus, Machiavelli believes that individual action has a constant and predictable pattern: how one behaves reflects the sort of psychological attributes that one has been granted. Machiavelli did not use a single term to denote 'character'. Rather, he alternated without apparent distinction between words such as *natura* and *qualità* to describe the personal traits which lie behind and guide human action. As Machiavelli observes in the *Ghiribizzi*, there are as many different temperaments and casts of mind given by nature as there are different faces. In part, he seems to subscribe to a naturalistic belief, common in the medical science of his day, about the effects of the bodily 'humors'. The differentiation between modes of human conduct is the result of different balances and mixtures of humors. Sometimes, as in the 'Tercets on Fortune' and 'The Ass', Machiavelli treats the humors as constitutive of individual characters and as occasionally requiring medical attention (such as purging) to set them right when they are out of kilter. More commonly, however, he applies the idea of humors to the nature of groups within the political community, in particular, to the nobility and the masses. In *The Prince*, the *Discourses*, and the *History of Florence*, he insists that cities or republics are always composed of a diversity of humors that induce the great men to seek preeminence over the common citizens and the people to desire freedom from the domination of the nobles. The persistent references to humors and related medical terminology would seem to suggest that Machiavelli believed that wholly naturalistic causes lay behind the behavior of specific persons as well as large populations.

Yet Machiavelli does not dismiss the role of education and environment either. He argues equally for the place of instruction and example in shaping the patterns of human conduct. In particular, he emphasizes the ability of human beings to learn how to conduct themselves through imitation of the behavior of others. Hence, in a republic, 'a good reputation and good example are of such an effect that men seek to imitate them, and the bad are ashamed to lead lives that go contrary to them' (D, 3.1; CW, p. 421). In principalities, political survival demands careful study of successful predecessors:

> Since men almost always walk in the paths beaten by others, and carry on their affairs by imitating – even though it is not always possible to keep wholly in the paths of others or to attain the ability of those you imitate – a prudent man will always choose to take the paths beaten by great men, and imitate those who have been especially admirable, in order that if his ability does not reach theirs, at least it may offer some suggestion.
>
> (P, 6; CW, 24)

Such passages clearly presume that the characteristics of men are susceptible to training and guidance by external sources. 'Imitation' implies constructive education. Machiavelli also

seems to assume that instruction shapes the collective characteristics found in the populations of different territories and nations.
He observes that 'human activity is at one time more efficacious
in this region than in that, and more in that than in this, according to the nature of the training from which the people acquire
their manner of life' (D, 3.43; CW, p. 521). The inhabitants of
particular countries acquire specific 'habits' and customs, in
effect national traits, which can be relied upon to shape and
condition their conduct. Machiavelli makes it clear that these
qualities, while ingrained and passed down from generation to
generation, are not inborn or inherent (he is not a nativist) but
the result of inculcation.

The most plausible conclusion is that Machiavelli never
evolved a systematic conception of the source of character, but
instead regarded it to be a somewhat loose and inspecific combination of nature and nurture. Yet regardless of his views on the
matter, his work proceeds from the premise that human beings
have deeply rooted psychological traits that require them to act
in a consistent and invariant fashion. As he remarks in 'The Ass',
'the mind of man, ever intent on what is natural to it, grants no
protection against either habit or nature' (CW, p. 725).
Machiavelli regards people to be essentially creatures of
patterned action. This comes out clearly in his descriptions of
the careers of various rulers. In chapter 19 of *The Prince*, which
traces the careers of a number of Roman emperors, Machiavelli
repeatedly refers to the qualities of particular rulers: some of
them governed on the basis of 'moderate' and 'humane' policies,
while others were 'cruel and rapacious' (P, 19; CW, pp. 70–6).
What they all shared in his account (the Roman emperor
Severus excepted) was a constancy of conduct, indicative of a
fixed quality. The fact that personal characteristics are usually
invariant he explains in one of two ways: 'either our natural
inclinations are too strong to permit us to change, or, because
having always fared well by acting in a certain way, we do not

think it a good idea to change our methods' (P, 25; CW, p. 91).
These factors are taken by Machiavelli as strong psychological
barriers to any variation in human conduct. The guiding hand
of character is so firm as to regulate action according to a clearly
charted course. This principle of nature is in turn invoked by
Machiavelli as the basis for his explanation of the ultimate
success and failure of rulers. It is precisely this dilemma that
animates much of his inquiry in *The Prince*. He comments in
chapter 25, 'I would observe that one sees a ruler flourishing
today and ruined tomorrow, without his having changed at all
in nature or quality' (P, 25; CW, p. 90). Machiavelli accounts
for this phenomenon with reference to the constancy of character. The problem, he says, arises in the relationship between
circumstances and character. When a ruler's character corre-
sponds to his circumstances, he will succeed in maintaining his
state and earning glory for himself. Should conditions change,
however, he is bound to fall from his position precisely because
his character no longer suits the times. Insofar as no one can be
expected to deviate from that course of action which appears
most 'natural' to him, Machiavelli must claim that rulers are
entirely subject to fortune to the extent that they possess invariant and permanent traits of character.

Machiavelli reaches essentially the same conclusion in the case
of republican leaders as in the case of the heads of principalities.
In the first book of the *Discourses*, he states succinctly that 'men
are born, live, and die, always, with one and the same nature' (D,
1.11; CW, p. 226). The third book returns to the problems posed
by the intractability of character in relation to changes of fortune.
He asserts the general proposition that the fortune of men
'depends upon whether their behavior is in conformity with the
times'; a person 'is likely to make fewer mistakes and to prosper
in his fortune when circumstances accord with his conduct, as I
have said, and one always proceeds as the force of nature compels
one' (D, 3.39; CW, p. 452). Thus, Machiavelli restates his funda-

mental psychological premise that the character which governs human behavior must match the situation in which the individual finds himself. In this connection, he mentions Pope Julius II (a name also prominent in *The Prince*), whose successes may be ascribed to the conformity of his conduct with the demands of the moment. But Machiavelli additionally cites the very painful example of his own political benefactor and friend Piero Soderini, whose ultimate failure is explained as a result of his 'good-natured and patient' character: 'So long as circumstances suited the way in which he carried on, both he and his country prospered. But when afterwards there came a time which required him to drop his patience and humility, he could not bring himself to do it, so that both he and his country were ruined' (D, 3.39; CW. p. 453). The irony of this observation is that Machiavelli himself – on the basis of the psychological principles he had already espoused in the *Ghiribizzi* in 1506 – might well have predicted the fate of Soderini. Machiavelli intimates as much in the *Discourses* when he claims that Soderini's 'patience and goodness' (especially in his treatment of the members of the Medici family) were his undoing: 'He lost together with his native city his position and his reputation' (D, 3.3; CW, p. 425). Yet, because character in Machiavelli's view is so thoroughly ingrained, there is no way that he might have deflected his friend from that path which the constancy of human psychology dictated. In the *Discourses* as in his other writings, the regulating effect of character on behavior has a dual foundation:

> First, it is impossible to go against what nature inclines us to. Second, having gotten well by adopting a certain line of conduct, it is impossible to persuade men that they can get on well by acting otherwise. It thus comes about that a man's fortune changes, for she changes his circumstances but he does not change his ways.

> (D, 3.9; CW, p. 453)

Nature and experience combine to create a fixed and unwavering character impervious to the vicissitudes of life. Regardless of circumstance, individuals can be expected to follow a consistent path in their actions. If they are lucky, their character will suit the times and they will succeed; otherwise, their failure is assured.

Attaining *virtù*

Machiavelli thus blames the fixity of human psychology for the ability of fortune to dominate and victimize humankind so completely. In Machiavelli's view, if men could dispense with a rigid set of character traits, if they could develop a flexibility of conduct, they would be able to conquer their conditions and to live as masters of their own fate. Machiavelli's model of such complete *virtù* may have been derived from the principles of military strategy that he later advocated explicitly in *The Art of War*. In that work, he emphasized the importance of flexibility and adaptation to the conditions found in the field. Machiavelli's mouthpiece Frabizio insists, 'You have to vary the form of the army according to the nature of the site and the nature and number of the enemy' (AW, 3; CW, p. 642). There can be no universally applicable battle plan and set of tactics. Rather, considering the full set of circumstances at the time of engagement and developing one's strategies in response to them represents the best approach to achieving victory. Machiavelli seems to have adopted the same general attitude in his conception of effective political leadership, which is unsurprising given his view that military prowess is the key to public affairs. Just as the successful field commander varies the array of his troops according to conditions, so Machiavelli sometimes seems ready to admit the possibility that the political leader (especially a prince) can 'vary his conduct as the winds of fortune and changing circumstances constrain him and ... not deviate from right conduct if possible, but be capable of entering upon the path of wrongdoing when this becomes necessary' (P, 18; CW, p. 66). This flexibility yields the core of the 'practical' advice that Machiavelli offers to the ruler seeking to maintain his state: exclude no course of action out of hand, but be ready always to perform whatever acts are required by political circumstance, regardless of their conformity with moral and religious expectations about the virtues appropriate to the 'good' ruler.

There is reason to believe, however, that Machiavelli himself had doubts about whether it was plausible to expect that human beings were psychologically capable of generating such flexible disposition within themselves. In spite of the great number of his historical examples, Machiavelli can point in *The Prince* to no single ruler who evinced the sort of variable *virtù* which he deems necessary for the control of fortune (Moses, with his friendship with God, perhaps comes closest). Rather, his case studies of successful rulers generally seem to offer instances of rulers whose characteristics suited their times and who (as in the case of Pope Julius II) 'would have been undone' if circumstances had changed (P, 25; CW, p. 92). Even the Emperor Severus, whose techniques Machiavelli lauds, succeeded because he employed 'the courses of action that are necessary for establishing himself in power'; he is not, however, to be imitated universally (P, 19; CW, p. 76). Machiavelli's short 'Life of Castruccio Castracani', a highly fictionalized biographical sketch of a fourteenth-century Luccese military commander (and opponent of Florence), is a case study in the strained relationship between fortune and human nature. Machiavelli suggests that Castruccio, who managed before his early death to unify a large part of Tuscany under his control, was favored by *Fortuna* with the conditions that suited his naturally martial character. Born humbly, Castruccio's military gifts were recognized early by his fellow citizens of Lucca and he rose quickly to become the de facto prince of the city. In his moment of greatest glory – a decisive defeat of the Florentine army – he catches cold and dies of a fever. Castruccio's story might appear to us to be a tale of success in overcoming fortune, at least until his death. But Machiavelli concludes otherwise. In a deathbed speech clearly fabricated by Machivelli himself, Castruccio says to his adoptive son and heir:

> If I had supposed, my son, that Fortune was going to cut off in the middle of my journey my path for moving on to that glory which I through my many successful actions hoped to attain, I would have toiled less and to you would have left, if a smaller state, fewer enemies and less envy … But Fortune, who is admitted to be arbiter of all human things, did not give me so much judgment that I could early understand her, nor so much time that I could overcome her.

(CW, p. 553)

Castruccio admits that he can see after the fact the failure of his enterprise because his nature led him to continue to engage in wars and to conquer territory, a policy that succeeded in the short run and showed no signs of turning. In fact, however, he remained the plaything of fortune, both because he could not foresee his own mortality and he did not fully anticipate the resentment that his victories would produce. Machiavelli leads us to conclude that Castruccio's military successes must be ascribed to nothing more than the suitability of his nature to the circumstances and that his downfall would have been inevitable had he survived. Castruccio simply lacked the flexibility of a prince endowed with the genuine qualities of *virtù* that would have guided him to adopt a less aggressive strategy, which would have yielded a smaller but stronger state instead of one that was large but 'weak and insecure' (CW, p. 553). In thrall to his own martial nature, Castruccio was both made and ruined by fortune, in Machiavelli's view.

In line with his observations about the limitations imposed by human nature in the face of fortune, Machiavelli's evaluation of the chances for creating a new, psychologically flexible type of character is extremely guarded. When speaking of the acquisition of *virtù*, he tends to employ hypothetical language: 'If it were possible to change one's nature to suit the times and circumstances, Fortune would not change', that is, one would always be successful (P, 25; CW, p. 91). The doubts implied by the grammar echo his more explicit pessimism in the *Ghiribizzi*:

> And truly, anyone wise enough to adapt to and understand the times and patterns of events would always have good fortune or would always keep himself from bad fortune; and it would come to be true that the wise man could control the stars and the Fates. But such wise men do not exist: in the first place, men are short-sighted; in the second place, they are unable to master their own natures; thus it follows that Fortune is fickle, controlling men and keeping them under her yoke.
>
> (MF, p. 135)

In the 'Tercets on Fortune', Machiavelli imagines that the true mastery of circumstances requires the ability to time perfectly the leap from one wheel of fortune to the next just as the first wheel turns downward and the other moves upward. Such adjustment to the whims of *Fortuna* is, however, deemed psychologically impossible:

> And since you cannot change your character nor give up the
>> disposition that Heaven endows you with, in the midst of
>> your journey she abandons you.
> Therefore, if this he understood and fixed in his mind, a man

> who could leap from wheel to wheel would always be
> happy and fortunate,
>
> but because to attain this is denied by the occult force that rules
> us, our condition changes with her course.
>
> (CW, p. 747)

Such observations must make us wonder whether Machiavelli's advice that princes acquire dispositions which vary according to circumstance was so 'practical' (even in his own mind) as he had asserted. His ambivalence in this regard may reflect that fact that, on the one hand, he recognized all too well the inadequacy of human psychology and behavior as an active force in political affairs, while, on the other hand, he could pose no solution to this challenge which did not violate the very psychological assumptions of fixed nature and character that he embraced.

The effect of the Machiavellian dichotomy between the need for flexibility and the inescapable constancy of character is to demonstrate an inherent practical limitation in single-ruler regimes. The reader is readily led to the conclusion that, just because human conduct is rooted in a firm and invariant character, the rule of a single man is intrinsically unstable and precarious. This reverses, of course, the widespread praise of the strength of monarchy (ranging from Aristotle's time to the Renaissance) on account of the permanence and reliability of royal virtue. St Thomas Aquinas, to mention but one example, argued that monarchy lessens the opportunity for unjust government to arise because government by a single, constant will affords the greatest assurance that a community will be ruled according to the common good. Conversely, regimes in which a group governs tend to fall into dissension and strife, according to Aquinas. The character of a single ruler is better known and more predictable than the qualities of some multitude of rulers.

Innovation in republics

Machiavelli provides a psychological argument to overturn the traditional preference for monarchy over populist regimes. In the *Discourses*, he points out how the psychology of human character tends to favor a republic over a principality, since the former 'is better able to adapt itself to diverse circumstances than a prince owing to the diversity found among its citizens' (D, 3.9; CW, p. 453). Machiavelli illustrates this claim by reference to the evolution of Roman military strategy against Hannibal. After the first flush of the Carthegenian general's victories in Italy, the circumstances of the Romans required a circumspect and cautious leader who would not commit the legions to aggressive military action for which they were not prepared. Such leadership emerged in the person of Fabius Maximus, who 'proceeded heedfully and cautiously, far from all impetuousity and all Roman boldness, and good fortune caused his method to fit well with the times' (D, 3.9; CW, p. 452). Yet when a more offensive stance was demanded to defeat Hannibal, the Roman Republic was able to turn to the leadership of Scipio, whose personal qualities were more fitted to the times. Neither Fabius nor Scipio was able to escape 'his habits and his customary conduct'; each 'acted through nature and not through choice' (D, 3.9; CW, p. 452). The fact that Rome could call on two types of temperaments at appropriate moment suggests to Machiavelli an inherent strength of the republican system.

> If Fabius had been king of Rome, he might easily have lost this war, since he was incapable of altering his methods according as circumstances changed. Since, however, he was born in a republic where there were diverse citizens with diverse dispositions, it came about that, just as it had a Fabius, who was the best man to keep the war going when circumstances required it, so later it had a Scipio at a time suited to its victorious consummation.

> (D, 3.9; CW, p. 452)

Changing events require flexibility of response, and since it is psychologically implausible for human character to change with the times, the republic offers a viable alternative: people of different qualities match different situations. It is extreme good fortune if a monarchic regime manages to generate even two good princes in a row. By contrast, 'for a republic this should be still more possible, since the method of choosing allows not merely two able rulers in succession but countless numbers to follow one another. Such a succession of able rulers will always be present in every well-ordered republic' (D, 1.20; CW, p. 246). The diversity of personal qualities characteristic of civic regimes, which had been reviled by Machiavelli's predecessors, proves to be an abiding advantage of republics over principalities.

In *The Art of War*, Machiavelli reinforces his conclusion about the usefulness of the variability of personality found in popular regimes. A central purpose of the work is to defend the claim that armies drawn from the ranks of citizens are best suited for military operations. One of his major reasons for advocating this position is that such militias are likely to contain both generals and soldiers who will not prove disruptive to the public order in peacetime. Professional commanders and their companies lack an occupation when no campaigns occur or are anticipated, but their skills qualify them for nothing but fighting. In the absence of the promise of pay, and with only their ability to wage war as their qualifications, they are likely to engage in robbery and to threaten the general domestic peace. Such a military professional is by nature and circumstance 'rapacious, fraudulent, violent, and must have many qualities which of necessity make him not good; nor can men who practice it as a profession, the big as well as the little, be of any other sort, because this profession does not support them in time of peace' (AW, 1; CW, p. 574). By contrast, the members of citizen armies have their 'normal' trades and interests to pursue, to which they will gladly and productively return when wartime ends. 'A city that uses its own forces, fears only its own citizens', Machiavelli remarks (AW, 1; CW, p. 585). Commanders and troops ought thus to be chosen among 'men who know how to live by some other profession', since 'each one of these will gladly make war in order to have peace, and will not seek to disturb the peace in order to have war' (AW, 1; CW, p. 578). The example of Rome is especially illustrative for Machiavelli:

> Rome, then, when she was well governed (which was up to the time of the Gracchi) did not have any solider who took up this pursuit as his profession, and for that reason she had few bad ones ... A well-ordered city will then decree that this practice of warfare shall be used in times of peace for exercise and in times of war for necesssity and for glory, and will allow the public alone to practice it as a profession, as did Rome. Any citizen who in such an activity has another purpose is not a good citizen, and any city that conducts itself otherwise is not well governed.
>
> (AW, 1; CW, p. 576)

In order to ensure this end, Rome rotated its legions and those who commanded them. When Rome abandoned this policy, however, it was ruined: once the city 'freely began to allow men chosen for those armies to practice soldiering as their profession, these men soon became arrogant', as a result of which the army itself began to dictate the course of the empire (AW, 1; CW, p. 578). Moreover, a citizen army has the advantage of permitting its leaders to draw upon a wide range of the skills possessed by its members beyond their military qualifications. Because such men will have considerable knowledge and experience necessary to maintain a fighting force in the field, 'it is useful to have plenty [from different occupations] because their skills can be applied to many things, and it is a very good thing to have a solider from whom you can get double service' (AW, 1; CW, p. 587). The principle at stake is the same as in the case of rotating republican leadership: since individual men possess a single fixed set of properties, and they thus are unable to adapt to circumstances that do not suit their characters, it is better to draw on a diverse body of citizens rather than to rely upon one sort only.

This does not mean that Machiavelli's confidence in the capacity of republican government to redress the political shortcomings of human character was unreserved. After all, he gives us no real indication of how republics manage to identify and authorize the leaders whose qualities are suited to the circumstances. It is one thing to observe that such variability has occurred within republics, quite another to demonstrate that this is a necessary or essential feature of the republican system. At best, then, Machiavelli offers us a kind of empirical generalization, the theoretical foundations of which he leaves unexplored. Indeed, the *Discourses* point out that republics have their own intrinsic limitation in regard to the flexibility of response needed to conquer fortune. Just as with individual human beings, for whom it is difficult (if not impossible) to change their personal characteristics, so 'institutions in republics do not change with the times ... but change very slowly because it is more painful to change them since it is necessary to wait until the whole republic is in a state of upheaval; and for this it is not enough that one man alone should change his own procedure' (D, 3.9; CW, p. 453). If the downfall of principalities is the fixed structure of human character, then a failing of republics is a devotion to the perpetuation of institutional arrangements that are no longer adequate to the conditions they confront.

Yet this limitation is perhaps not so damaging to republics as the fixity of human psychology is to principalities, since in Machiavelli's view republican government enjoys a unique foundation absent in every other type of regime. In the first book of the *Discourses*, Machiavelli explains the difference

between republics and other types of constitution. He initially
enumerates six basic forms of government:

> Some who have written about states say that they have one of
> three kinds of government, called principality, aristocracy, and
> democracy ... Some other, and many think, wiser men hold
> that there are six kinds of government, of which three are very
> bad; the three others are good in themselves, but so easily
> corrupted that even they come to be pernicious ... For princi-
> pality easily becomes tyrannical; aristocracy with ease becomes
> oligarchy; democracy without difficulty changes itself into
> anarchy.

> (D, 1.2; CW, pp. 196–7)

All of these varieties of government, Machiavelli claims,
emerged 'by chance among men', who at first lived 'scattered in
the fashion of the beasts' until they decided to gather into a
community 'so that they could better defend themselves', with
the strongest and most courageous man chosen as a leader (D,
1.2; CW, p. 197). A sense of what is good and what is wicked
soon developed, and laws and punishments were laid out. Over
time, the people began to accept a hereditary rule, rather than
choosing for themselves; from this the rulers easily slipped into
tyranny. The great men of the community eventually gathered
the strength to overthrow the tyrant and ruled according to law
at first; however, their descendents likewise were seized by
avarice and ambition, and the aristocracy devolved into an
oligarchy. The masses grew tired of this iniquitous rule and
overthrew the oligarchs, setting up a democratic government in
their place. The laws of this regime were not respected for long
either, however, and anarchy ensued, 'in which there is no fear
either of private or of public men, so that since each lived as he
pleased, every day a thousand wrongs were done' (D, 1.2;
CW, p. 198). In an attempt to curtail the chaos of anarchy, a

principality was once again established, and the cycle started afresh.

Machiavelli readily admits the problems inherent in this process of continual rise and collapse. In fact, he argues, the result of such frequent corruption and resulting rebellion is that states are continually unstable and fall victim to their stronger neighbors: 'Almost no state can have so much life that it can pass many times through these shifts and continue on its feet. But it probably happens that, as it struggles, a state ... becomes subject to a neighboring power that is better organized' (D, 1;2; CW, p. 199). The only way out of this dilemma, Machiavelli maintains, is achieved by an innovation, namely, the creation of a mixed form of government:

> I say, then, that the said types of government are pestiferous, by reason of the short life of the three good and the viciousness of the three bad. Hence, since those who have been prudent in establishing the laws have recognized this defect, they have avoided each one of these kinds by itself alone and chosen one that partakes of them all, judging it more solid and more stable, because one keeps watch over the other, if in the same city there are principality, aristocracy and democracy.

> (D, 1.2; CW, p. 199)

The idea that republicanism provided a means to balance the elements of society, and thus to break out of the continuous cycle of degeneration, collapse, and rejuvenation was, of course, not original; it echoed the arguments found in works such as Polybius' *Histories* and Cicero's *De res publica*. But unlike classical authors, Machiavelli views the introduction of republican 'mixed' government as a purely human invention, an institution designed by men to redress the inconveniences endemic to all other forms of rule.

In some cases, republics are the creation of a single man, a lawgiver, such as Solon in Athens and Lycurgus in Sparta. Rome's republic, by contrast, emerged as the result of a more developmental process to which many men contributed over a long course of time. First, when its kings were overthrown, the nobility retained a monarchic element (in the form of the Consuls) while mixing in an aristocratic dimension (the Senate). When the nobles eventually became too overbearing, a popular or democratic component (the Tribunes) entered the Roman system of government as well:

> And so favorable to her was Fortune that even though she passed from the government of the king and aristocrats to that of the people ... yet never, in order to give authority to the aristocrats, did she take all authority away from the kingly element, nor did she remove entirely the authority of the aristocrats to give it to the people, but continuing her mixed government, she was a perfect state.

> (D, 1.2; CW, p. 200)

The balance between the three different interests in the state endowed the Roman Republic with a large measure of vitality and longevity that other regimes were unable to match. By giving weight to each of the classes, Rome was able to stave off the vicious cycle of decay and reform to which most regimes are subject; its institutions are, therefore, worthy of profound admiration. In turn, Rome's greatness is ascribed by Machiavelli not merely to 'good fortune and military vigor', although he does not deny the importance of these factors (D, 1.4; CW, p. 202). Rather, Rome achieved and maintained a successful republic because it was populated by so many good citizens who were able, as circumstances dictated, to adjust the institutions of government to redress grievances in order to stave off rebellion and constitutional change. The Roman Republic sustained itself as an expression of the collective ingenuity of many generations of its members, stimulated, Machiavelli believes, by 'the disunion between the plebians and the Senate' (D, 1.2; CW, p. 200). (The latter point will be taken up at more length in chapter 5.)

As wholly human creations, republics enjoy a special property that distinguishes them from all other constitutional forms, namely, their capacity to be reenergized and set back on the right path when they become corrupt. Machiavelli stresses this point at the beginning of the third book of the *Discourses*. Since republics (and especially Rome) 'possess some goodness by means of which they gain their first reputation and their first growth', they are particularly susceptible to 'changes ... to their advantage that take them back toward their beginnings. And therefore those are best organized and have longest life that through their institutions can often renew themselves or that by some accident outside their organization come to such renewal' (D, 3.1; CW, p. 419). Machiavelli identifies two methods for achieving this goal of renovation: by man and by law. The former denotes the presence in the republic of an individual of noteworthy excellence, who 'with his striking words and his vigorous actions' stimulates his fellow citizens to emulate him and to adopt his modes of conduct (D, 3.1; CW, p. 420). Ancient Rome had many such men who came along at regular intervals and inspired its denizens to act for the sake of the collective good of the republic rather than for personal gain, as had occurred during the time of its founding. The attainment of renewal by means of law pertains to the creation of political institutions and statutes that attempt to recapture the public-spiritedness of earlier days, either by punishing those who place self-interest above the common welfare or by inventing offices that 'opposed the ambition and pride of the citizens' (D, 3.1; CW, p. 420). Again, Rome excelled at this for much of its history, as Machiavelli copiously documents with reference to such innovations as the Tribunes and the Censors as well as public prosecutions of notorious offenders. Both means are useful in reminding citizens of their duties and drawing them away from the temptations of 'growing wicked and acting in a more dangerous and lawless fashion', to which men are naturally prone (D, 3.1; CW, p. 421). Indeed, Machiavelli speculates that had some combination of renewal by men and by law occurred 'at least every ten years' in Rome, the 'necessary result would have been that Rome would never have become corrupt' (D, 3.1; CW, p. 421). In other words, by persistent acts of renewal, the flux caused by the turning wheels of fortune can be controlled and overcome. By means of a well-ordered and often regenerated republic, men collectively afford themselves a way out of the dilemma posed by their dual subservience to *Fortuna* and to their own psychologies.

Of course, Machiavelli fully realizes that such renewal – at least if it is the result of internal events, rather than compelled by external necessity – cannot be assured, and thus republics do grow corrupt and moribund, as Rome did during the final century of the Republic. But given that in republics, any one of a large number of men may achieve regeneration by example or by reform, it remains at least in principle possible that they will be able to return to their good roots, in comparison with any other mode of political life. The best that we can conclude from Machiavelli's comments about the renewal of republics, especially when examined in conjunction with his treatment of the psychology of human character, is studied ambivalence. He understands all too well the devastating political consequences (at least in principalities) of the possession of ingrained personal qualities. Yet he offers no compelling reason to believe that human beings can conduct themselves other than with reference to constant and firmly rooted traits. He employs his psychological principles to criticize the monarchic form of government in comparison with the republican constitution, but he provides no assurances that republics will reliably convert their advantage in psychology into an advantage in politics. Human ingenuity is always potentially efficacious against the force of the heavens, but success is never guaranteed. The hand of *Fortuna* remains an inescapable and unpredictable factor in the life of republics no less than principalities.

4
Violence/law

Readers of Machiavelli have long noted, and have often been troubled by, the primacy of violence in his work. His model of politics places heavy emphasis on force, strength, and military prowess. *The Prince* asserts that the 'good foundations' of political order are two-fold: 'Good laws and good armies. And because there cannot be good laws where armies are not good, and where there are good armies, there must be good laws, I shall omit talking of laws and shall speak of armies' (P, 12; CW, p. 47). In the *Discourses*, likewise, Machiavelli states that 'the foundations of all states is good military organization, and that where this does not exist there cannot be good laws or good anything else' (D, 3.31; CW, p. 500). Republics no less than principalities demand that the ability to fight be foremost among the qualifications for success in the public realm. Is Machiavelli's insistence upon the centrality of violence in political life simply a reflection of his experiences in the Florentine government as an advisor on military affairs? Certainly, his intimate knowledge of warfare (reflected, for instance, in *The Art of War* as well as in the many reports and letters he wrote during his time in the service of Florence) shaped his views about the role of martial strength as a precondition of the success of states and individual leaders. Yet Machiavelli's nearly obsessive foregrounding of the violent dimensions of politics is fundamentally based on the broader features of his conception of the human condition and the circumstances that determine the outcome of political events.

The priority of force

In particular, as Machiavelli consistently upholds throughout his writings, the importance of military strength is intimately connected to the proposition that citizen militias yield the most reliable form of armed forces. The citizen body itself must be trained and prepared to fight for the state. From the Thebans to the Romans to the English of his own day, Machiavelli says, successful governments have ensured that their citizens possess the skills necessary to engage in warfare whenever the need arises (D, 1.21; CW, pp. 246–7). Relying upon armies composed of foreign troops (whether those of mercenaries or allies) constitutes a recipe for defeat or servitude. For Machiavelli, an armed populace, properly instructed in the tactics of warfare, ensures the independence of the state. Indeed, he regards a public militia as the cornerstone of any hope a state might possess of warding off the vicissitudes of *Fortuna*: 'If, then, a city is armed and organized like Rome, and every day her citizens, both individually and in public, have occasion to test their ability and the power of Fortune, always in whatever weather they will have the same spirit and keep the same dignity. But when they are unarmed and rely on the rapid motions of Fortune and not on their own strength and wisdom, they will vary as she varies' (D, 3.31; CW, p. 501). Civic military prowess is judged by Machiavelli to afford an effective counterweight to the persistent threat posed by fortune.

To understand Machiavelli's fascination with physical force as an indispensable tool of politics, then, it is necessary to relate it to both his cosmology and his psychology. As we have seen in his discussion of *Fortuna* in chapter 25 of *The Prince*, he proposes two analogies for understanding the human situation in the face of events. Initially, he asserts that fortune resembles 'one of our destructive rivers which, when it is angry, turns the plains into lakes, throws down the trees and buildings, takes earth from one spot, puts it in another; everyone flees before the flood; everyone yields to its fury and nowhere can repel it'. Yet the furor of a raging river does not mean that its depredations are beyond human control: before the rains come, it is possible to take precautions to divert the worst consequences of the natural elements. 'The same things happen about Fortune', Machiavelli observes (P, 25; CW, 90). *Fortuna* may be resisted by human beings, but only in those circumstances where 'strength and wisdom' have already prepared for her inevitable arrival. Machiavelli reinforces the association of *Fortuna* with the blind strength of nature by drawing a connection directly to the goddess's gender. Commenting that success depends upon appreciation of how *Fortuna* works, he explains in *The Prince* that his own experience has taught him that 'it is better to be impetuous than cautious, because Fortune is a woman and it is necessary, in order to keep her under, to beat and maul her' (P, 25; CW, p. 92). The feminine identity of *Fortuna* demands an aggressive, even violent response, lest she take advantage of those men who are too retiring or effeminate themselves to dominate her.

These dual themes of the domination of nature and the physical mastery of woman are also present in the 'Tercets on Fortune'. The gendered aspect of *Fortuna* receives greater attention there than in *The Prince*, yet the connection to nature (in the form of the 'rapid torrent') is also expressed (CW, p. 748). *Fortuna* is implicated by Machiavelli in a dialectic of violence. On the one hand, she treats human beings with great cruelty: 'Her natural power for all men is too strong and her reign is always violent ... You cannot trust yourself to her nor hope to escape her hard bite, her hard blows, violent and cruel' (CW, pp. 744, 747). *Fortuna* attacks human beings wantonly and without provocation; she is, in effect, a wild animal, incomprehensible to those who try to treat her on human terms. On the other hand, she is not beyond manipulation by the man who ably interprets her ways and applies his knowledge to the goal of domination. 'If prowess (*virtù*) still greater than hers does not vanquish her', then *Fortuna* will prevail (CW, pp. 747–8). Yet this is not the necessary result. 'We well realize how much he pleases Fortune and how acceptable he is who pushes her, who shoves her, who jostles her' (CW, pp. 748–9). Violence begets violence: if she is forceful with human beings, then the appropriate response is to adopt her stratagems. A bold man, unafraid to meet *Fortuna* on her own terms, stands at least a chance of victory. Throughout his corpus, the goddess is depicted as a primal source of violence (especially as directed against humanity) and as antithetical to reason. *Fortuna*'s apparent irrationality, demonstrated by the fickle treatment of human beings, is at the same time the token of a violent character. No amount of reason can compel *Fortuna* to 'come to her senses', because the basis of her existence is overwhelmingly violent. Words will never suffice as a means of controlling *Fortuna*: people, if they have any hope of turning the goddess to their bidding, must act directly to resist her machinations. And that active response to *Fortuna* must itself be of a violent sort.

Yet the role of violence in politics depends upon the sort of regime that is under consideration. In the case of the prince, the struggle with fortune is a personal one, requiring the acquisition of certain individual traits that are unnecessary in the case of republican government. For a prince to respond effectively to *Fortuna*, success depends upon him setting aside the distinctively human aspects of his nature and becoming bestial. As Machiavelli observes in *The Prince*,

> There are two ways of fighting: one according to the laws, the other with force. The first is suited to man, the second to animals; but because the first is often not sufficient, a prince must resort to the second. Therefore, he needs to know well how to put to use the traits of animal and of man … A prince needs to

know how to adopt the nature of either animal or man, for one without the other does not secure him permanence.

(P, 18; CW, pp. 64–5)

No other reaction than beating and mauling is available to the prince faced with an angry, menacing, and entirely implacable foe. Yet this passage also implies that another form of conflict is conceivable, one that accords with law. Such a route is characteristic, in particular, of republics, which afford a public sphere that permits rational discussion within a legal framework for Machiavelli. A republican government depends primarily upon a citizen body composed of those who engage in reasoned speech and who thus eschew bestial violence in preference for verbal sparring. It is true that Machiavelli upholds the necessity of a citizen militia and of class strife as preconditions of a free republic. In this sense, his insistence upon the primacy of 'good arms' over 'good laws' is sustained. But the republic differs from the principality in an important regard: in the former, arms are subsumed under law and conflict is socialized in order to achieve common goals, whereas the latter depends upon regular doses of violence in order to overcome fortune. Republican, as contrasted with princely, regimes (at least those that are well ordered) do not depend on public violence or the purely coercive character of social institutions.

Why does the predicament encountered by the prince differ from that of the republic? Princes, or at any rate those who come to power through their own deeds, must confront the unreliability of the population over whom they rule. In part, this is the result of the generally self-interested character of human nature. As discussed in chapter 3 above, Machiavelli regards people to be more concerned about their own immediate advantage than about the good of others, such that a prince should never count upon anyone (including, and perhaps especially, those who have supported him in the past) to be loyal to him. Thus, for the prince to retain control over his subjects, he must employ strategies that will induce them to accede to his power, most notably by keeping them fearful by establishing firmly in their minds the possibility that he will engage in acts of cruelty. Citing one of his favorite examples of effective princely rule in his own times, Machiavelli remarks, 'Cesare Borgia was thought cruel; nevertheless that well-known cruelty of his re-organized the Romagna, united it, brought it to peace and loyalty' (P, 17; CW, p. 61). Consequently Machiavelli proposes one of his best-known maxims for princely government: 'it is much safer for a prince to be feared than loved, if he is to fail in one of the two.' He explains this precept by direct reference to the self-interested nature of men:

> While you do well by them they are all yours; they offer you their blood, their property, their lives, their children … when the need is far off; but when it comes near you they turn about. A prince who bases himself entirely on their words, if he is lacking in other preparations, fails … Men have less hesitation in injuring one who makes himself loved than one who makes himself feared, for love is held by a chain of duty which, since men are bad, they break at every chance for their own profit; but fear is held by a dread of punishment that never fails you.
>
> (P, 17; CW, p. 62)

This theme runs across the text of *The Prince*. Danger and downfall await a ruler who places too great a trust in the support of subjects, particularly in difficult times. History is rife with examples of such ill-starred princes, who, imagining themselves worthy of the love of the people as an adequate safeguard against misfortune, find that their judgment leads to their destruction. To safeguard himself, then, 'a prince, in order to hold his position, must acquire the power to be not good, and under-stand when to use it and not use it, in accord with necessity'

(P, 15; CW, p. 58). This is the core of the moral flexibility that Machiavelli associated with *virtú*, whether or not he believed that any person could actually attain it fully.

To be sure, Machiavelli is aware that the use of violence or the threat of violence against one's subjects entails certain risks. He distinguishes, specifically, between 'good' and 'bad' uses of cruelty. The former requires the prince to employ violence soon upon his ascension with 'a single stroke' against selected enemies for as brief a period of time as possible. This will instill fear in subjects, yet will do little real harm and will pacify the populace. Cruelty badly used runs the opposite direction, increasing over time and rendering the prince less secure in his grasp on power. 'Injuries are to be done all together, so that, being savored less, they will anger less', Machiavelli advises (P, 8; CW, p. 38). 'A wise prince, then, is not troubled about a reproach for cruelty by which he keeps his subjects united and loyal because, giving a few examples of cruelty, he is more merciful than those who, through too much mercy, let evils continue' (P, 17; CW, p. 61). He holds up Agathocles, king of Sicily, and Liverotto of Fermo as two resplendent examples of cruelty who succeeded in subduing their realms by organizing and conducting the murders of fellow citizens. Yet because their violent acts (which Machiavelli acknowledges to be wicked) suited the circumstances they confronted, they achieved their goals. On account of the appropriateness of their techniques, 'Agathocles and others like him, after countless betrayals and cruelties, could for a long time live safely in their native places and defend themselves from foreign enemies, and the citizens never plotted against them' (P, 8; CW, p. 38). Their violent deeds obtained them power precisely on account of the fact that they understood how to act cruelly as conditions demanded.

Yet Machiavelli admits that some forms of violence are to be avoided at all costs, because they will never produce a positive outcome for the prince. For example, a successful ruler 'refrains from the property of his citizens and from their women ... men forgot more quickly the death of a father than the loss of a father's estate ... So long as the great majority of men are not deprived of property or honor, they are satisfied' (P, 17, 19; CW, pp. 62–3, 67). Hence, Machiavelli's counsel about the use of violence by princes is always circumscribed by his view of the generally self-interested nature of human beings. The effective ruler, whose own self-interest is directed by his desire to maintain and extend his hegemony, must constantly calculate how to manipulate the self-seeking impulses of the populace at large. When such precepts are broken, Machiavelli notes, the ruler no longer engenders fear in his people, but rather hatred. This is to be avoided at all costs, he emphasizes: 'the wise prince is careful ... to avoid everything that makes him hated and despised, and any prince who avoids that does what is needed, and in other kinds of bad repute encounters no danger' (P, 19; CW, p. 67). Subjects who hate their prince will look for every opportunity to oppose him, a situation from which only disaster awaits. Hatred encourages plots and conspiracies against the ruler, which arise when men think that they have less to lose by taking up arms against him than by obeying him. If a prince is feared but not hated, anyone who seeks to eliminate him will have a difficult time gathering together a group of co-conspirators numerous enough to succeed in the task, since subjects will not wish to endanger their positions by incurring the wrath of the leader should the plot fail. The calculation changes in the case of the hated ruler, however, since a vast number of his people will judge him so harshly that they will gladly run any risk to remove him from power.

These considerations concerning the application of violence by the prince are further complicated, according to Machiavelli, by the group interests that exist within societies. In addition to conduct deemed 'rapacious', namely, the seizing of 'the property and the women of his subjects', the prince undermines his own power by disaffecting the popular segment of the community, whose support (especially their participation in the civil militia) he needs (P, 19; CW, p. 67). It is a general principle of Machiavelli's thought that the populace in all states is divided between the noble elites, who are wealthy and power seeking, and the masses, who wish to avoid oppression. In this regard, the nobles and the masses have interests that are usually antithetical and irreconcilable. Machiavelli maintains that princely rulers succeed only when they enjoy the confidence of at least one of these groups. Ideally, 'well-ordered states and wise princes with the utmost attention take care not to make the rich desperate and to satisfy the people and keep them contented; this matter is very important for a prince' (P, 19; CW, p. 70). Yet given how difficult it is to satisfy both at once in light of their conflicting goals, rulers may be compelled to make a choice between the two, in which instance Machiavelli leaves no doubt whom they ought to prefer: the popular segment. It is far easier for a ruler to make do without the elites than the people. In his view, should the prince depend on the nobles and then lose their support, he can expect that they are likely to act against him and replace him with another leader (P, 9; CW, pp. 40–1). By contrast, the backing of the people, who are more deferential, serves to check against elite opposition: 'The prince's strongest resource against conspiracies is not to be hated by the masses, because always a conspirator believes that by the death of a prince he will please the people. But when he believes he will anger them, he does not gather courage to undertake such a plan' (P, 19; CW, p. 68). It is also presumably the case that the masses, who lack the 'perception' and 'shrewdness' of the elites (P, 9; CW, p. 40), will be more easily deceived by the prince into believing that he has their best interests at heart.

In general men judge more with their eyes than with their hands, since everybody can see but few can perceive.

> Everybody sees what you appear to be; few perceive what you
> are, and those few dare not contradict the belief of the many,
> who have the majesty of the government to support them …
> the mob is always fascinated by appearance and by the outcome
> of an affair; and in the world, the mob is everything; the few
> find no room when the many crowd together.
>
> (P, 18; CW, pp. 66–7)

Machiavelli consequently urges rulers to engage in dissembling
their true characters and intentions, on the grounds that 'so
simple-minded are men and so controlled by immediate necessities that a prince who deceives always finds men who let
themselves be deceived' (P, 18; CW, p. 65). Indeed, *The Prince*
offers numerous suggestions for how such deceit of the masses
may be accomplished. By contrast, nobles are more likely to see
through the ruse and to employ their discovery as grounds to
oppose him.

Containing conflict

Machiavelli thus evinces in *The Prince* deep ambivalence, even
studied cynicism, about the worth of the popular elements of the
community. On the one hand, the endorsement of the masses is
indispensable to the maintenance of the ruler's power. He
clearly will fail if he lacks their backing. On the other hand,
Machiavelli harbors no illusions about the political savvy of the
people: they can readily be fooled by a prince who works hard
to combine a fearful demeanor with a reputation worthy of their
awe and praise. In the *Discourses*, however, his view of the
masses is far more positive and hopeful, largely on account of the
differences that exist between republics and principalities. Recall
that in *The Prince* Machiavelli distinguished between two forms
of conflict – one lawful and humane, the other requiring bestial

force. He insisted that the prince must gear himself to fight as an animal. In a republic, on the contrary, the path of law comes to the fore. In the *Discourses*, he reiterates the position of *The Prince* concerning the social cleavage between the nobles and the masses, but draws a noticeably different conclusion. He invites his readers to consider

> that in every republic there are two opposed factions, that of the people and that of the rich, and that all the laws made in favor of liberty result from their discord ... Nor can a republic in any way reasonably be called unregulated where there are so many instances of honorable conduct; for these instances have their origin in good education; good education in good laws; good laws in those dissensions that many thoughtlessly condemn. For anyone who will properly examine their outcome will not find that they produced any exile or violence damaging to the common good, but rather laws and institutions conducive to the public liberty.

> (D, 1.14; CW, p. 203)

A republic has a different set of goals than a principality; the former seeks liberty together with dominion, whereas the latter aims at security, as shall be addressed in chapter 5. As a result, each system has distinct means of achieving its proper end, such that the division between the elite and popular factions (and the role played by government in mediating between them) takes on a unique complexion depending on the context. Principalities succeed only when they are ruled by individuals who are able to employ techniques they have learned from the ferocity of beasts in order to induce fear in the hearts of citizens. Well-ordered republican institutions tame the conflicts between elite and mass without necessary recourse to the animalistic dimensions of force.

It must be emphasized that Machiavelli does not mean to imply that republics ought to eliminate or suppress conflict between nobility and people. Comparing Rome to Venice and Sparta, he points out that the latter two cities, to the extent they maintained republican regimes while largely removing sources of public contention, lacked vitality and the potential for growth. By contrast, Rome, which invited internal dissention by arming all its citizens and incorporating foreigners, developed into a vigorous commercial and military power. Given Machiavelli's decided preference for imperial dominion – a subject to which we shall return in the next chapter – he concludes that 'it is necessary ... to give scope to disturbances and discords among the inhabitants, as well as one can, because without a large number of men, and well armed, a republic never can grow larger, or, if it does, never can maintain itself' (D, 1.6; CW, p. 209). In his view, there is no middle course between stability and dispute: the choice is between calm stagnation, on the one hand, and conflictual expansion, on the other. There is no doubt in Machiavelli's mind which approach affords the best model for republics:

> I believe the Roman method must be followed, and not that of other states, because to find a course half way between one and the other I believe is not possible. Those enmities rising between the people and the Senate must be borne, being taken as an evil necessary to the attainment of Roman greatness.
>
> (D, 1.6; CW, p. 211),

In particular, a republic that socializes the conflicts between mass and elite factions is more open to change and thus better able to adapt itself to changing circumstances, and especially to military threats and opportunities. An armed and inclusive society such as Rome possesses citizens who are prepared to act and sacrifice in times of war, while disarmed and insular peoples prove 'effeminate or divided' when confronted with conditions that call for military prowess (D, 1.6; CW, pp. 210–11).

It should be evident that Machiavelli's preferred version of republican government involves a notable stress upon the role of the popular element within the community. Indeed, one of the central aims of the *Discourses* is the defense of the view that the active involvement of ordinary citizens forms the best safeguard of civic liberty as well as the most reliable source of decision-making about the public good. In particular, Machiavelli contrasts the constancy and trustworthiness of the masses, who are often accused of fickleness and ineptitude, with the improbity of the nobles, who are commonly regarded to be the 'natural' leaders of a republic. The example of Rome is especially instructive for him. He observes that 'if one will look at the purposes of the nobles and those who are not noble' in Rome, 'there will be seen in the former great longing to rule, and in the latter merely longing not to be ruled, and as a consequence greater eagerness to live in freedom' (D, 1.5; CW, p. 204). The collective character of the common people, in other words, is less grasping and more amenable to serving the public good than that of the nobility. What permitted Rome to avoid public corruption and to extend its empire for so many centuries, Machiavelli believes, was precisely the fact that the masses demanded and were gradually accorded such a large hand in public determinations. Machiavelli says that while some people regard the evolution of the Roman constitution to be the cause of 'the ruin of Rome', as the office of the Tribune was created and as non-nobles gained access to 'all the other offices in the city government', in reality the flexible and adaptable character of the Republic's institutions reflected an extension of liberty that ultimately benefited the entire populace (D, 1.5; CW, p. 205). The people thwarted the use by patricians of public power to pursue private interests. Machiavelli draws the conclusion that 'if the common people are set up to guard liberty, it is reasonable that they will care for it better, and since they cannot seize it themselves, they will not allow others to seize it' (D, 1.5; CW, p. 205). The apparent 'tumults' between the popular and elite segments of the Roman population were in fact the key to Rome's success.

Words and laws

What gives Machiavelli the confidence to view republican citizens so differently from subjects of a prince? One important factor supporting Machiavelli's praise for the role of the people in securing the republic is his belief in the generally illuminating effects of public speech upon the citizen body. Near the beginning of the first *Discourse*, he notes that some may object to the extensive freedom enjoyed by the Roman people to assemble, to protest, and to veto laws and policies. But he responds that the Romans were able to maintain liberty and order because of the people's ability to discern the common good when it was shown to them. At times when ordinary Roman citizens wrongly supposed that a law or institution was designed to oppress them, they could be persuaded that

> their beliefs are mistaken … [through] the remedy of assemblies, in which some man of influence gets up and makes a speech showing them how they are deceiving themselves. And as Tully says, the people, although they may be ignorant, can grasp the truth, and yield easily when told what is true by a trustworthy man.
>
> (D, 1.4; CW, p. 203)

The reference to 'Tully' (that is, the Roman republican statesman, orator, and philosopher Marcus Tullius Cicero) confirms that Machiavelli has in mind here a key feature of classical republicanism: the competence of the people to respond to and support the words of the gifted orator when he speaks truly about the public welfare. Machiavelli does not dispute his earlier finding in *The Prince* that the masses are less perspicacious than the elites, but he asserts that they possess a measure of common sense that affords them the competence to evaluate the validity of various plans of action that are laid before them. By contrast, in a princely regime, in which secrecy, deception, and force are necessary techniques of rule, the people enjoy no comparable chance to demonstrate their collective capacity to make judgments about the public weal. Republican institutions frame the opportunity for the masses to display the traits they nascently possess.

Machiavelli returns to this theme and treats it more extensively at the end of the first *Discourse*. In a chapter intended to demonstrate the superiority of popular over princely government, he argues that the people are well ordered, and hence 'prudent, stable and grateful', so long as room is made for public speech and deliberation within the community. Citing the traditional Roman formula *vox populi, vox dei* ('the voice of the people is the voice of God'), Machiavelli insists that

> general opinion possesses marvelous power for prediction … As to judging things, very seldom does it happen, when a people hears two men orating who pull in opposite directions, that if the two are of equal ability the people does not adopt the better opinion and does not understand the truth of what it hears.

> (D, 1.58; CW, p. 316)

Not only are the people competent to discern the best course of action when orators lay out competing plans, but they are in fact better qualified to make decisions, in Machiavelli's view, than are princes. For example, the people can never 'be persuaded that it is wise to put into high places a man of bad repute and of corrupt habits – something that a prince can be persuaded to do easily and in a thousand ways' (D, 1.58; CW, p. 316). Likewise, should the people depart from the law-abiding path, they may readily be convinced to restore order: 'an uncontrolled and rebellious people can be spoken to by a good man and easily led back into a good way. A wicked prince nobody can speak to, and the only remedy is steel ... for the curing the people's disease words are enough, but for the prince's disease steel is required' (D,1.58; CW, p. 317). The contrast Machiavelli draws is stark. The republic governed by words and persuasion – in sum, ruled by public speech – is almost sure to realize the common good of its citizens; and even should it err, recourse is always open to further discourse. Non-republican regimes, because they exclude or limit discursive practices, ultimately rest upon coercive domination and can only be corrected by violent means.

By no means, however, does Machiavelli's confidence in the masses translate into a wholesale endorsement of populism or democracy. He admits that 'sometimes good decisions are not made in republics', because 'the people, deceived by a false image of the good, many times desire their own ruin' (D, 1.53; CW, pp. 303, 302). Specifically, the masses, unlike the elites, tend to rush too quickly to support policies that appear to produce immediate and obvious rewards:

> Therefore, considering when it is easy and when it is hard to get a people to accept something, one can make this distinction: either what you are trying to persuade them of shows on its surface gain or loss; or the decision to be made seems coura-geous or cowardly. When in a plan put before the people, gain is apparent, even though loss be hidden beneath, and when it seems courageous, even though the ruin of the republic be hidden beneath, always the multitude is easily persuaded to approve.
>
> (D, 1.53; CW, p 303)

Consonant with his general conception of human nature, self-interest and the promise of quick profit readily attract the untutored in particular, and afford an opportunity for leaders to manipulate the populace for private benefit. Yet Machiavelli points out that this is a double-edged sword. While the people may be induced by corrupt men to authorize plans that 'cause the fall of the republic' and 'the ruin of the city, there also results – and more often – the ruin of the citizens put at the head of such an undertaking, because after the people have counted on victory, and loss comes, they accuse neither Fortune nor the weakness of him who managed it, but his wickedness and ignorance'. As a consequence, 'death or prison or exile' generally awaits a popular leader who persuades the masses to engage in foolhardy endeavors (D, 1.53; CW, p. 305). Even if too late to save their liberty, the people retain the capacity to discover that they have been fooled and to take harsh measures against their deceiver. This lesson should by itself serve as a caution against the rashness of republican leaders in their advocacy of policies.

Machiavelli believes that such disaster for republics may be avoided, however, by institutional means that render the leading men of the city responsible and accountable for their words and deeds. The establishment of the office of the Tribune of the Plebs in republican Rome serves as his exemplar of how to achieve the goal of reining in the powerful. Machiavelli explains that the Tribune was a product of necessity emerging from the conflicts between nobles and elites once the latter had gained sufficient self-assurance that they attempted to oppress the latter. So long as the people could place their trust directly in the civic virtue and public spiritedness of the nobility, no such magistrate was required, since 'where without law a thing of itself works well, law is not necessary, but when such a good custom is lacking, at once law is necessary' (D, 1.3; CW, p. 202). Note Machiavelli's emphasis on legislation, which, as we have seen, he juxtaposes to outright violence as the typically 'human' and republican means for containing conflict: the institution of the Tribune was an example of innovative legislative action on the part of Rome, in the face of necessity, to stave off a crippling wave of violent clashes. On the one hand, the office would not have been created without 'much confusion, uproar and danger of civil war from the dissensions between the people and the nobility'; on the other hand, once empowered, the Tribunes were endowed 'with such position and such dignity that always thereafter they were the middle-men between the people and the Senate, able to head off the arrogance of the nobles' (D, 1.3; CW, p. 202). Circumstances posed an opportunity for the Romans to demonstrate their ability to adapt by means of institutional design and to introduce a check on the arbitrary conduct of the elites. Without such ingenuous recourse to new laws, for which Machiavelli praises the Roman Republic throughout the *Discourses* and elsewhere, the dynamic that energized the city would have been lost.

The main function of the tribunal office was public prosecution of those denizens of Rome, specifically the nobles, who sought to hold sway over and oppress the people and hence to derail republican institutions. Machiavelli says that when a lawful means to hold such men accountable is available, 'the citizens, for fear of being accused, do not attempt things against the state; and if they do attempt them, they are put down instantly and without favor ... Therefore nothing makes a republic so firm and solid as to give her such an organization that the laws provide a way for the discharge of the partisan hatreds that agitate her' (D, 1.7; CW, p. 211). The significance of the emphasis on lawfulness should not be lost. Law constitutes the pre-eminent safeguard against the destruction of republican government due to the outbreak of open violence:

> When there are no lawful methods, unlawful ones are resorted to; and without doubt the latter produce much worse effects

than do the former. Because if a citizen is oppressed by lawful means, even though injury is done to him, little or no disorder in the republic comes of it ... if they are done with public forces and means, which have their definite limits, they do not go on to something that may destroy the republic.

(D, 1.7; CW, p. 212)

Machiavelli imagines what might have occurred in Rome had the office of the Tribune not existed to prosecute Coriolanus: 'the mob would have killed him if the Tribunes had not cited him to appear to defend his case' (D, 1.7; CW, p. 212). Machiavelli is no friend of mob rule, to be sure, but he can envisage no alternative without a legal method of ensuring the accountability of public authorities. Indeed, he points to the absence of such institutional mechanisms as a fatal flaw of Florence's republican government, which permitted powerful men to plot its overthrow because there was no way to bring them up on charges and punish them.

Machiavelli recognizes, of course, that a danger lurks within a political system that permits open accusations against its leading men, namely, that slanders may ensue and the prosecutorial function may be abused. By whipping up the people with lies about political opponents, an aspiring oppressor is afforded an effective instrument for building his own partisan support. Yet Machiavelli concludes that slander is generally most common and most harmful in republics 'where that [method] of lawful charges is used least and where cities are least organized to deal with them' (D, 1.8; CW, p. 216). As a remedy for the ill effects of slander, he proposes that its commission as well as malicious prosecution should be included among the activities for which citizens may legitimately be penalized:

Hence the organizer of a republic ought to arrange that charges can be brought against any citizen in it, without any fear and without any hesitation. And when a charge has been made and well investigated, slanderers should be severely punished. They cannot complain when they are punished, since places are open for hearing complaints against those whom they slander in the public arcades.

(D, 1.8; CW, p. 216)

In the absence of such susceptibility to public recourse against slander, Machiavelli claims, aggrieved citizens will turn to private and violent means to receive satisfaction. This is exactly what transpired in Florence, according to him, with the result that the partisanship became so extreme that the city was ruined. In Rome, by contrast, where citizens were 'obliged to make charges according to law', and to accept the consequences if they proved to be false, Machiavelli finds a reasonable legal way of heading off rampant slander (D, 1.8; CW, p. 217). Properly constituted within a republic, a system of law can control and hem in the outbreak of public violence.

The implementation of legislation capable of regulating the dangers of social conflict endemic to republics indeed reflects one of the potential strengths of their constitutions, namely, their capacity to adjust to circumstances in a way that appears psychologically impossible in principalities. It is for this reason that Machiavelli rails against critics of Rome who express horror at the perceived chaos that came from the assignment to the masses of such a large measure of authority. He insists that any harm done by the refusal of ordinary Roman citizens to go to war, or even by 'disorderly running through the streets, locking of the shops, the people all leaving Rome', was far outweighed by the beneficial outcome of legal and institutional change that resulted (D, 1.4; CW, p. 203). By according the masses outlets for pursuing their ambitions and aspirations, the Roman Republic, and those states that adopt its general constitutional program, prove far more capable of sustaining their civic organization than under systems in which the people are either oppressed or entirely manipulated. Machiavelli teaches that the free republic is not achieved and maintained without cost or danger, but it is more in accord with human nature and less bestial than the political alternatives. By permitting the populace at large the role of the driving force in change that redresses grievances, republican government demonstrates itself to be prepared to meet new difficulties posed by the fluctuations of fortune in ways unavailable to the rule of individual princes or small oligarchic groups. While granting to the people the preponderance of ultimate responsibility for the exercise of political power may never ensure a state's success or even survival, since such assurance does not fall within the ambit of the limited faculties of mortal humans, it is demonstrably more reliable than any other constitutional order devised by humankind.

5
Security/liberty

Are republics really better than principalities? It seems that for Machiavelli this question admits of no unqualified resolution. To some extent, the changing circumstances dictated by fortune mean that the judgment of which political system is 'better' depends upon which one is more suited to the conditions in which a state finds itself. While Machiavelli sometimes expresses special admiration for republics, and he often demonstrates the strengths of republican regimes in comparison with principalities, as we have noted in preceding chapters, his broad worldview simply does not permit him to endorse a single system of government without reservation and for all times. Indeed, to do so would violate one of his key insights that the vicissitudes of fortune demand the complete flexibility of political institutions. The answer, in particular, revolves around the posing of an additional question: what are the respective purposes and strengths of each type of government? That is, what distinctive goals do principalities and republics respectively seek to achieve and what are the effects when those aims are attained?

Machiavelli consistently and clearly distinguishes between a minimal and a full conception of 'political' or 'civil' order, thus positing a diversity of possible ends that might be sought within public life. A minimal constitutional order, found in a properly organized principality, is one in which subjects live securely (*vivere sicuro*), ruled by a strong government which holds in check the aspirations of both nobility and people, but is in turn balanced by other legal and institutional mechanisms. Such regimes are especially well suited for maintaining stable government within fixed territories. In a fully constitutional regime, however, the goal of the political order is the freedom of the community (*vivere libero*), created by the active participation of, and contention between, the nobility and the people. Only in a republic may this goal be attained. In turn, free republics (especially if arranged along the lines suggested by the Roman example) are particularly adept at military conquest and territorial expansion. Throughout his writings, Machiavelli takes care to distinguish between these two very different sets of purposes and consequences. Moreover, he evaluates specific historical instances of regimes according to their success at attaining the goals inherent to them, yet without declaring unconditionally that one goal is always to be preferred to another. If Machiavelli ultimately prefers a republic, and thus deserves to be credited with the status of a profoundly republican thinker, his endorsement depends upon his belief that liberty is necessary in order to acquire empire and that imperial expansion is the most praiseworthy result of politics.

Secure monarchy

That security is the primary and most desirable attainment of principalities is evident throughout *The Prince*. The key issue posed about princely government, according to Machiavelli, pertains to the methods employed in acquiring and retaining power in a state in such fashion that the inhabitants (people and nobles) accept the authority of their ruler and obey him without opposition. Such stability is summarized by his oft-repeated insistence that the sole aim of a prince ought to be to 'maintain his state'. From the outset, he distinguishes between two divergent forms of principality: those that are 'hereditary, where their rulers have for a long time been princes', and those that are 'new', that is, in which no dynastic foundation for government exists (P, 1; CW, p. 11). Of the two sorts of princely rule, Machiavelli believes that the security of the hereditary type is relatively unproblematic:

> I say, then, that hereditary states accustomed to the family of their prince are preserved with many fewer difficulties than are new states; the prince needs only not to go beyond the customs of his forefathers, for otherwise he can let time take care of what happens. Thus, if such a prince uses ordinary care, he always retains his position unless some unusual and excessive force deprives him of it ... A prince by birth has fewer reasons and less need for giving offence than does a new ruler. Hence an established prince will certainly be better loved, and if excessive vices do not make him hated, it is reasonable that his people will naturally wish him well.
>
> (P, 2; CW, p. 12)

Indeed, the relative stability afforded by heredity leads Machiavelli to concentrate the main thrust of his advice in *The Prince* on 'new' rulers, who cannot fall back on family lineage and long-standing custom, but who instead encounter many difficulties and challenges in establishing themselves and holding their states securely.

Machiavelli's counsels about managing the conflicts between the nobility and the masses, avoiding conspiracies, organizing and leading armies, and employing violence and deceit, which make up the bulk of *The Prince*, are explicitly directed toward new leaders. The absence of dynastic legitimacy means that a new prince can only succeed when he uses the innovative tactics (associated with *virtù*) advocated by Machiavelli, by which 'he makes himself secure enough if he avoids being hated and despised, and keeps the people contented with him – which he needs to attain, as I have said at length above' (P, 19; CW, p. 68). By contrast, *virtù* does not seem to be necessary for the hereditary ruler to maintain his position in safety, since he possesses other resources (apparently not subject to the extreme fluctuations of fortune) on which to draw. The new prince's aim, then, should be to adjust his conduct so as to establish himself on the model of hereditary rule:

> The things written above, carried out prudently, make a new prince seem like an old one, and make him quickly safer and firmer in his position than if he were in it by right of descent. Because the actions of a new prince are more closely watched than those of a hereditary prince, and when those reveal strength and wisdom, they lay hold on men and bind them to him more firmly than does ancient blood.
>
> (P, 24; CW, p. 88)

Consequently, new princes who succeed in their plans by adopting Machiavelli's recommendations will enjoy the same advantages as hereditary rulers and additionally will deservedly receive praise for having accomplished this feat entirely as a result of their own efforts without depending upon the legitimacy conferred by ancestry. But a broader point should not be missed in this remark: whereas the new prince attains the safe occupation of his office only with great difficulty (and perhaps not at all, given Machiavelli's remarks noted in previous chapters about the implausibility of acquiring complete *virtù*), the hereditary monarch finds himself in a decidedly superior position. In this sense, a well-ordered hereditary kingdom constitutes the paradigmatic case of the best form of principality.

Machiavelli's writings illustrate this view with specific reference to the political arrangements of France, for which he offers repeated and effusive praise. The French state in the early sixteenth century was already well on its way toward the structures that would yield the classic absolutist regime one hundred years later. Throughout his work, but especially in the *Discourses*,

Machiavelli lauds the contemporary French monarchy for its well-regulated character, its constitutionality, and its success at calming the feudal chaos of earlier centuries. During his career as a secretary and diplomat in the Florentine republic, Machiavelli came to acquire vast experience of the inner workings of French government. He was intimately involved in negotiations between Florence and the French crown in order to maintain the alliance between the two on which the republic's protection rested. Moreover, he wrote several short treatises on topics related to the cultural and social traditions, as well as political structure, of France. These experiences with the French monarchy were transplanted into his substantial treatment in the more theoretical tomes composed by Machiavelli.

Perhaps the most distinctive feature of Machiavelli's analysis of France is his examination of the relationship between the socio-economic and political factors that shaped French society. His initial foray into the understanding of France may be found in his 'Ritratto di cose di Francia' ('Account of French Affairs', hereafter referred to as the 'Ritratto'), which was probably completed while he was still in the service of Florence in 1510 or 1511. In the 'Ritratto', Machiavelli correlates the status of the French 'crown and king' – which he calls the 'strongest, richest and most powerful' monarchy of the time – with the circumstances of both the nobility and the popular segment of society (HFOS, p. 1). He recognizes that the conditions obtaining in France resulted from the dynastic failure, and consequent elimination at the end of the Middle Ages, of most of the independent, fragmented baronies that had long prevented establishment of the hegemony of the crown. As the reversion of land and rights occurred, French kings wisely assigned baronial titles to members of their own blood line, thus cementing the loyalty of a previously unruly, uncooperative and disruptive nobility. In particular, Machiavelli remarks, even the most distant members of the royal family, established in their own fiefdoms, were motivated to obey the king in the hope (however dim) that they or their progeny might someday inherit the throne (HFOS, p. 2).

The barons, in turn, directly aid the king in maintaining his authority over the people; what he ordains, the magnates execute (HFOS, p. 8). The French subjects have, in any case, developed habits of deference, obedience, and humility toward the Crown and the nobles. France enjoys a great abundance of natural resources, Machiavelli observes, yet the common people live humbly and avoid ostentation; neither do they threaten to revolt against the Crown or bear a grudge against the monarchy (HFOS, pp. 4, 7). Nor is the nobility especially wealthy by more cosmopolitan standards; but the great men of the realm appear satisfied with their incomes, permitting the king to accumulate the largest share of the riches in the nation (HFOS, pp. 4, 8–10). While these socio-economic conditions are conducive to a tranquil kingdom, Machiavelli does not think they bode well for a successful army. Although praising the valor of the nobility, whose lesser sons diligently prepare to fight, he points out that the people are unfit to man the infantry. The king dare not arm them, lest they be given a chance to act upon their resentment toward the nobles who directly govern the populace. Since the king cannot depend upon his own subjects to fight in his army, he must turn to mercenaries, who are costly and unreliable (HFOS, pp. 2–3). On Machiavelli's account, the military is the only significant weakness of the French kingdom.

The 'Ritratto' evidently provided the source material for the appraisal of French government and society on display in Machiavelli's later work. Many of its observations recur, although now placed in a developed and sophisticated theoretical framework. Given that France is a hereditary monarchy, Machiavelli makes relatively little comment about its organization in *The Prince*. (Instead, we shall see that he incorporates most of his analysis of the topic into the *Discourses*. There are also some references to the circumstances of France in several other writings, such as 'A Discourse on Remodeling the Government of Florence' and *The Art of War.*) What discussion does occur in *The Prince* summarizes Machiavelli's previously stated attitude toward the strengths of the French regime. He recognizes that the power of the king of France derives from his relationship with the barons, with whom he enjoys an enduring connection that guarantees their partial independence even as they assist him in governing the subjects. In such a system, we find that

> there is a prince, with the barons who hold their rank not through the ruler's favor but through their ancient blood. Such barons as these have states and subjects of their own, who acknowledge them as their lords and have for them a natural affection ... The King of France is placed amidst a long-established multitude of lords acknowledged by their own subjects and loved by them; such lords have their vested rights; these the king cannot take from them without danger to himself.
>
> (P, 4; CW, pp. 20–1)

Consequently, Machiavelli contends that this general means of arranging political rule is so successful that should 'the country of France' come under foreign attack, the state 'can only be held with great difficulty' by its putative conquerors (P, 4; CW, p. 21). In France, then, the unity of the ruling elite is the source of royal strength.

Such strength is explicitly praised in chapter 19 of *The Prince*. In the context of substantiating the claim that the wise prince strives neither to harass the magnates nor to disturb the contentment of the people, Machiavelli states, 'The kingdom best organized and governed, in our times, is France' (P, 19; CW, p. 70). He returns to the observation of the 'Ritratto' concerning the social foundations of French rule, this time pointing to the role of the Parlement (the national system of courts) in deflecting the resentment of both the nobility and the people toward the crown. In France, he says,

> There are numberless good institutions on which depend the king's liberty and security. Among these, the first is the Parlement and its authority. The organizer of that kingdom, knowing the ambition of the powerful and their arrogance, judged a bit in their mouths necessary for controlling them; and, on the other side, he knew the hatred of the masses for the rich, founded on fear; yet when planning to give both classes security, he did not permit their safety to be the king's special duty, in order to free him from the hatred he would incur from the rich for favoring the people, and the people for favoring the rich. Therefore, he set up a third body as judge, who, without any blame for the king, was to beat down the rich and favor the humble.

(P, 19; CW, p. 70)

Parlement functions as an intermediary institution, defending the masses against the nobility, without direct royal involvement. 'Nothing could be better or more prudent than this law, or a greater cause of security to the king and kingdom' (P, 19; CW, p. 70). The genius of the French political system stems from the ability of the king to rule effectively by keeping both people and nobility in check and arousing the direct hostility of neither.

Beyond the novelty of his observation about Parlement, which receives no substantial attention in the 'Ritratto', the passage in *The Prince* constructs a clear link between the kingdom of France and the goal of security. Security, as a matter of domestic, rather than foreign, concern, connotes the safety of the prince as the result of deference on the part of his subjects, which forms a central topic of concern for Machiavelli. As indicated already, his many remarks in *The Prince* stress that monarchic government – whether that of a hereditary ruler or a 'new' prince – must place security at the top of its priorities in order to achieve glory. An insecure royal regime – one in which either the nobility or the people or both have the capacity and desire to strike out against one another or their prince – will quickly and inevitably fail. 'A wise prince takes care to devise methods that force his citizens, always and in every sort of weather, to need the government and himself', Machiavelli declares, 'and always then will they be loyal' (P, 9; CW, p. 42). Only that ruler who discovers and employs the appropriate methods of controlling his subjects – dampening down their passions and ambitions, or at any rate, directing them toward the interests of the state – stands a chance of overcoming the vicissitudes of *Fortuna*. This is the heart of security, as Machiavelli understands it. Clearly, he holds in *The Prince* that the French monarchy had, in his own day, succeeded beyond any other regime in achieving this goal.

Machiavelli's most extensive remarks about the French king and kingdom are found in the *Discourses* rather than *The Prince*. At first glance, this might seem odd. Why would Machiavelli effusively praise (let alone even analyze) a hereditary monarchy in a work supposedly designed to promote the superiority of republics? The answer stems from Machiavelli's aim to contrast the best case scenario of a monarchic regime with the institutions and organization of a republic. Even the most excellent monarchy, in Machiavelli's view, lacks certain salient qualities that are endemic to well-ordered republican government and that mark the unique purposes for which the latter constitution is best suited. While Machiavelli's treatment of France in the *Discourses* echoes some of the themes touched upon in the 'Ritratto' and *The Prince*, he also introduces important new elements into the analysis. In particular, he asserts that the greatest virtue of the French kingdom and its king is the dedication to law. France is 'more tempered by the laws than any other kingdom of which we have notice in our times', Machiavelli declares (D, 1.58; CW, p. 314). The presence of law, as we have already seen, is also an essential ingredient of well-ordered republics; it distinguishes regimes that have a constitutional basis from those subject to either sheer force or license. But the legal order of the French constitution operates in a different way than (and toward a distinct end from) the laws in the Roman Republic. Once again, Machiavelli highlights the 'mediating' function of the Parlement. 'The kingdom of France', he states, 'lives under laws and regulations more than any other kingdom' because such legal order is maintained by 'the parlements ... and most especially that of Paris' (D, 3.1; CW, p. 422). The primary result of the authority of Parlement is the regeneration of the French traditions and customs that rein in the powerful: 'They are renewed by it every time it prosecutes a prince and rules against the king in its decisions. Up to now it has held its own because it has been a firm enforcer of law against the nobility' (D, 3.1; CW, p. 422). Moreover, Machiavelli immediately notes that the failure of Parlement to continue to exercise control over the powerful men of the kingdom would lead to the rapid decay and destruction of the entire French state. These passages of the *Discourses* seem to suggest that Machiavelli has great admiration for the institutional arrangements that obtain in France. Specifically, the French king and the nobles, whose power is such that they would be able to oppress the populace, are checked by the laws of the realm which are enforced by the independent authority of the Parlement. Thus, opportunities for unbridled tyrannical conduct are largely eliminated, rendering the monarchy temperate and 'civil'.

Limits of security

Yet such a regime, no matter how well ordered and law-abiding, remains incompatible with public freedom and *vivere libero*. Discussing the ability of a monarch to meet the people's desire for liberty, Machiavelli comments that in regard to the 'popular wish of having their freedom again, since the prince cannot satisfy it, he should investigate what the reasons are that make them wish to be free' (D, 1.16; CW, p. 237). He concludes that a few individuals want freedom simply in order to command others; these, he believes, are of sufficiently small number that they can either be eradicated or bought off with honors. By contrast, the vast majority of people confuse liberty with security, imagining that the former is identical to the latter: 'But all the others, who are countless, wish freedom in order to live in security (*vivere sicuro*)' (D, 1.16; CW, p. 237). Although the king cannot give such liberty to the masses, he can provide the security that they crave:

> Those others, for whom it is enough to live securely, are easily satisfied by the making of ordinances and laws which provide for the general security and at the same time for the prince's own power. When a prince does this and when the people see that under no circumstances will he break those laws, in a short time they feel secure and contented. An example is the kingdom of France, which lives safely for no other reason than that those kings are restrained by countless laws in which is included the security of all her people. And he who organized that state planned that about arms and money the kings should do as they wish, but that they could deal with nothing else except as the laws prescribe.

> (D, 1.16; CW, pp. 237–8).

Machiavelli's larger point here is that the law-abiding character of the French regime ensures security, but that security, while desirable, ought never to be confused with liberty. This is the limit of monarchic rule: even the best kingdom can do no better than to guarantee to its people tranquil and orderly government.

Indeed, the establishment of security constitutes the very purpose of principalities, which is why Machiavelli holds France in such high esteem. The people of France are servile, but they remain contended under hereditary rule and thus pose no danger to its stability.

Machiavelli maintains that one of the consequences of such a stable form of princely constitution is the disarmament of the people, which is the major token of their servility. Reiterating in the *Discourses* the observation he made in the 'Ritratto', he comments that 'the king of France, with so great a kingdom', nonetheless 'lives as a tributary' to foreign mercenaries.

> This all comes from having disarmed his people and from having preferred ... to enjoy an immediate profit, to be able to plunder the people, and to escape an imagined rather than a real danger, instead of doing things that would give them security and make their states happy forever. This bad policy, if sometimes it does produce some years of quiet, is in time the cause of want, of damage, and of destruction that cannot be remedied.

> (D, 2.30; CW, p. 410)

A state that makes security a priority cannot afford to arm its populace, for fear that the masses will employ their weapons against the nobility (or perhaps the crown). Yet at the same time, such a regime is weakened irredeemably, since it must depend upon foreigners to fight on its behalf. In this sense, any government that takes the secure life as its goal generates a passive and impotent populace as an inescapable result. By definition, such a society can never be free in Machiavelli's sense of *vivere libero*, and hence is only minimally, rather than completely, political or civil.

Confirmation of this interpretation of the limits of principality for Machiavelli may be found in his further discussion of the disarmament of the people, and its effects, in *The Art of War*. He addresses there the familiar question of whether a citizen army is to be preferred to a mercenary one, concluding that the liberty of a state is contingent upon the military preparedness of its subjects. Acknowledging that 'the king [of France] has disarmed his people in order to be able more easily to command them', Machiavelli still concludes that 'as to the error that the King of France makes in not keeping his people disciplined for war ... such a policy is a defect in that kingdom, for failure to attend to this matter is the one thing that makes her weak' (AW, 1; CW, pp. 584, 586–7). In his view, whatever benefits may accrue to a state by denying a military role to the people are of less importance than the absence of liberty that necessarily accompanies such disarmament. The problem is not merely that the ruler of a disarmed nation is in thrall to the military prowess of foreigners. More crucially, Machiavelli believes, a weapons-bearing citizen militia remains the ultimate assurance that neither the government nor some usurper will tyrannize the populace. 'So Rome was free four hundred years and was armed; Sparta, eight hundred; many other cities have been unarmed and free less than forty years' (AW, 1; CW, p. 585). Machiavelli is confident that citizens will always fight for their liberty – against internal as well as external oppressors. Indeed, this is precisely why successive French monarchs have left their people disarmed: they sought to maintain public security and order, which for them meant the elimination of any opportunities for their subjects to wield arms. The French regime, because it seeks security above all else (for the people as well as for their rulers), cannot permit what Machiavelli takes to be a primary means of promoting liberty.

Machiavelli's dim opinion of French military strength, especially in fighting overseas campaigns of conquest, is expressed particularly in *The Prince*'s analysis of the failure of King Louis XII's adventures in Italy, which Machiavelli observed at close range. He enumerates a panoply of reasons that

Louis's expedition lacked success, some of which had to do with poor strategic decisions directly attributable to his lack of military and diplomatic good sense. But other elements of Machiavelli's explanation stem from the tensions inherent in the organization of French government. In earlier times, the French monarchy had succeeded in consolidating control over territories that nominally acknowledged its authority because pre-existing conditions favored its claims:

> Those states which, after they are acquired, are united to an old state belonging to him who gains them, are either in the same region and of the same language or they are not. When they are, it is very easy to retain them, especially when they are unused to living in freedom; to hold them securely, the conqueror needs only to wipe out the line of the prince who was ruling them, because as to other things, if their old conditions are preserved and their customs are not diverse, men continue to live quietly. This is true of Burgundy, Brittany, Gascony and Normandy, which have been for a long time with France; and though in language they differ somewhat from her, nevertheless their customs are the same, so they get on easily with one another.
>
> (P, 3; CW, pp. 13–14).

Northern Italy proved quite a different case. First, its language and customs were widely divergent from that of the French and thus not amenable to easy integration into what Machiavelli terms a 'mixed' principality (P, 3; CW, p. 12). Second, the Italians of Lombardy had tasted freedom and so were not inclined to submit themselves to the servility that the French expected and demanded of their populace. Third, and of greatest damage, France's excessive reliance on alliances and on mercenary forces, in the absence of home-grown troops trained and prepared to fight on his behalf, undermined Louis's ability to assert a formidable military presence that might have kept the Italians in fear of his government. In short, however secure the French monarchy might be in its home territories, the qualities required to sustain an imperial presence in Italy were doomed precisely by those strengths that made France a formidable domestic power. The quest for empire stretched beyond limit the capabilities of the greatest principality that Machiavelli had encountered in his own times. The organization that produced security in France constrained that regime's pretensions to extend its sway over other nations.

The case of France's military weakness as an imperial force illustrates a larger difference between minimally constitutional systems exemplified by the French principality and fully political communities such as the Roman Republic, namely, the conse-quences of the conflicts between classes within the society. In France, as Machiavelli insists, the common people were entirely passive and the aspirations of the nobility were largely held in check by the institutions of the state. As a result, security is achieved. By contrast, in a well-ordered republic, where the realization of liberty is the paramount goal, both the people and the nobility take an active (and usually clashing) role in self-government. The liberty of the whole, for Machiavelli, depends upon the desire for liberty asserted by its component parts. The Roman Republic represents to him the quintessential instance of this principle. In his discussion of the foundations of Roman greatness in the *Discourses*, Marchiavelli remarks, 'I say that those who condemn the dissentions between the nobility and the people seem to me to be finding fault with what as a first cause kept Rome free, and to be considering the quarrels and the noise that resulted from those dissensions rather than the good effects they brought out' (D, 1.3; CW, p. 202). Machiavelli knows that he is adopting an unusual perspective here, since customarily the blame for the collapse of the Roman Republic had been assigned to warring factions that eventually ripped it apart. He is not unmindful that 'the controversies between the people and the Senate ... continued until the time of the Gracchi, when they caused the ruin of free government' (D, 1.6; CW, p. 207). There is a persistent danger in republics that in-fighting between the classes will break out into the open violent pursuit of contrary interests. Machiavelli admits in the *History of Florence* that 'the serious and natural enmities between the people and the nobles, caused by the latter's wish to rule and the former's not to be enthralled, bring about all the evils that spring up in cities; by this opposition of parties all the other things that disturb republics are nourished' (CW, p. 1140). In the case of Florence, the division between the nobles and the masses generated destructive disunity. But Machiavelli holds that precisely the same conflicts generated a 'creative tension' that was the source of Roman liberty and the occasion of Rome's greatness. Rome was 'disunited', but 'because the Roman people's desire was more reasonable' – they wanted only to avoid oppression, rather than to attain equality, as in Florence – 'their injuries to the nobles were more endurable, so that the nobility yielded easily and without coming to arms; hence, after some debates, they agreed in making a law with which the people would be satisfied and by which the nobles would remain in their public offices' (CW, p. 1140). Conflict between the two main classes is unavoidable, but it can be socialized through the range of means that Machiavelli describes in both the *Discourses* and the *History of Florence*, including public debate, adherence to law, and rigorous military training of citizens.

Republican liberty

As we have discussed already, Machiavelli expresses particular confidence in the capacity of the common people to contribute to the promotion of communal liberty. In the *Discourses*, he ascribes to the masses a quite extensive competence to judge and act for the public good in various settings, explicitly contrasting the 'prudence and stability' of ordinary citizens with the unsound discretion of the prince (D, 1.58; CW, p. 316). 'A people that commands and is well organized will be just as stable, prudent, and grateful as a prince', Machiavelli insists, 'and if there is any superiority, it is with the people' (D, 1.58; CW, p. 315). The reason for this, he maintains, is that the people are more concerned about, and more willing to defend, liberty than either princes or nobles. Where the latter tend to confuse their liberty with their ability to dominate and control their fellows, the masses are more concerned with protecting themselves against repression by the nobility and consider themselves 'free' when they are not abused by the more powerful or threatened with abuse. In turn, when they fear the onset of such oppression, ordinary citizens are more inclined to object and to defend the common liberty. An active role for the people, while necessary for the maintenance of vital public liberty, is fundamentally antithetical to the hierarchical structure of subordination-and-rule on which monarchic security rests. The preconditions of living freely simply do not favor the maintenance of the quietude that forms the aim of constitutional monarchy.

Machiavelli also contrasts the contained conflict found in Rome with an alternative republican model (realized in ancient Sparta and in latter-day Venice), which tends toward the suppression, rather than the expression, of the popular segment of society. As Machiavelli describes them, both Sparta and Venice were small and 'closed' societies in which, by policy, new inhabitants were discouraged or entirely prevented from settling. Consequently, he claims, power could be entrusted to a few men (whether Spartan elders or a civic oligarchy) without rancor or the fear that they would oppress their fellow citizens, since such people were few, scattered, and largely undisturbed by government.

> He who defends the Spartan and Venetian arrangement says that
> those who put the guardianship in the hands of the powerful do
> two good things: one is that they satisfy their ambition better,
> for, having a share in the republic – since they have this club in
> their hands – they have reason to be satisfied better; the other
> is that they take away from the restless spirits among the people
> a sort of authority that is the cause of numberless quarrels in a
> republic and likely to bring the nobility to a state of desperation
> that in time will bring forth evil effects.
>
> (D, 1.5; CW, p. 205)

Peace and quiet are the hallmarks of such regimes, in which the ruling groups 'had no better means to hold their office firm than to keep the people secure from every injury. As a result, the people had no fear and did not desire authority. And not having authority and not being afraid, the strife they might have had with the nobility and the reason for rebellions were taken away; and they could live united for a long time' (D, 1.6; CW, p. 208). While such republics are constitutional orders, inasmuch as legal precepts limit the power of their governors, they do not aspire to any higher aim than to establish and enforce security, much as principalities. In this sense, although governments such as those found in Sparta and Venice may earn some praise from Machiavelli (as does France), he clearly believes that their organization betrays the potentialities implicit in the republican system for achieving full public freedom and for enjoying the fruits of this liberty.

Specifically, Machiavelli believes that republics that are secure but circumscribe the liberty of the people are poorly prepared when opportunities for growth and expansion (and hence, riches and glory) are thrust upon them. Indeed, in his view, such a government does everything it can to remain small and insular, even to the point of adopting a 'constitution or law' forbidding it 'to grow greater ... Because expansion is the poison of such republics, he who organizes them ought in all possible ways to prohibit their making conquests, because such conquests, based on a weak state, are its total ruin' (D, 1.6; CW, p. 210). It may indeed be the case that republics on the order of Sparta and Venice are able to last for centuries intact and relatively stable, but this is a sign of their weakness rather than their strength. Machiavelli draws an explicit contrast to Rome: 'either you are talking of a republic that wishes to set up an empire, like Rome, or of one to which it is enough to remain itself. In the first case it is necessary to do everything as Rome did; in the second, Venice and Sparta can be imitated' (D, 1.5; CW, p. 205). The direct consequence of the pursuit of liberty as it occurred in Rome is, then, the establishment of the appropriate social and political conditions for the extension of territory and control. According to Machiavelli, 'love for free government springs up in people, for experience shows that cities never have increased in dominion or riches except while they have been at liberty' (D, 2.2; CW, p. 329). Domestic arrangements profoundly shape the ability of all governments, and especially republics, to succeed in the quest for military conquest as well as permanent empire.

Machiavelli cites a number of reasons why the well-ordered republic, the citizens of which are reliable defenders of liberty, affords the best chance for the realization of imperial pretensions. In general, a populace that loves liberty will be vigorous in its pursuit and thus prepared to struggle for a public good greater than the sum of private or partial interests. Any detriment to particular citizens will be judged secondary to the general well-being. Machiavelli explains that

> not individual good but common good is what makes cities great. Yet without doubt this common good is thought important only in republics, because everything that advances it they act upon, and however much harm results to this or that private

citizen, those benefited by the said common good are so many
that they are able to press it against the inclination of those few
who are injured by its pursuit.

(D, 2.2; CW, p. 329)

Machiavelli expressly contrasts this republican penchant for
public valor with the situation under a prince, who, seeking his
own profit first and foremost, either is unwilling to extend his
authority to new territories or else undermines his own security
(and that of his state) by engaging in conquests that will cause
discontent at home and danger abroad. Republican liberty
engenders a dynamic capacity in populations: they grow, their
riches multiply, and their citizens believe that they will be able
to enjoy the fruits of their gains. Servile populations, on the
other hand, harbor no such expectations and thus become
dispirited and dissolute – in short, corrupt.

Machiavelli contends, in turn, that expansion in republics, or
at any rate in those that follow the pattern of Rome, reinforces
and further invigorates the liberty that constitutes the source of
imperial success. This is true for several reasons. A well-ordered
republic does not merely conquer and reduce to the status of
slaves or slaughter the inhabitants of the territories that its armies
vanquish (at least if they were previously free peoples). Rather,
on the Roman model, a wise republic incorporates its former
enemies into its civilian population 'by keeping the ways open
and safe for foreigners who wish to come and live in it, in order
that everyone may live there gladly' (D, 2.3; CW, p. 334).
Hence, Rome 'obtained many associates, who in most respects
lived under the same laws as herself', and who were thus rapidly
integrated into the state (D, 2.4; CW, p. 337). Although the
Roman people did not surrender their leadership role in the
empire they acquired, they were able to amass an army of still
greater size, drawn now from the provinces as well as the city,
which provided an even more formidable foe capable of yet

greater conquests. Machiavelli contrasts this to the policy decreed in Sparta, which actively banned relations with foreigners, forbidding intermarriage, the conferral of citizenship, and commercial exchange, 'so that the city never could increase its inhabitants' (D, 2.3; CW, p. 335). Consequently, although Sparta possessed a well-trained and courageous military, its territories never enlarged and so the number of its troops never expanded.

Ultimately, Machiavelli's argument for the superiority of tumultuous republics of the Roman variety over either French-style monarchy or even other republican models stems from his belief, drawn from the lessons of history and experience, that they are better equipped to deal with the vicissitudes of fortune and to succeed in expansion and conquest. France and Sparta may have lasted longer, but neither achieved the wealth, glory, and honor enjoyed by Rome. Of course, one may object that Machiavelli's reasoning has troubling militaristic or even imperialistic overtones. Consequently, we may properly debate whether the expansionistic consequences of *vivere libero* are truly to be preferred to the *vivere sicuro* offered by a constitutional monarchy or stable republic. But that is a different question than asking what Machiavelli himself prized most highly. A free regime for him constituted a more valuable human political achievement, if only because such a system of self-government distinguished itself most obviously by its ability to expand its boundaries and to include increased amounts of territory under its rule.

Reception/reputation

At the hour of Niccolò Machiavelli's death in June 1527, there was little reason to suppose that his name would linger for five hundred years as one of the most significant figures in the history of Western thought. He had been a moderately successful Florentine statesman, who, when political circumstances turned against him, reinvented himself as an author of works on military affairs and history and as a popular, although not prolific, playwright. Machiavelli had rubbed shoulders with many great and powerful men, and he was well regarded by some of them, but most of his plans and dreams had been rebuffed or ignored. The Machiavelli known publicly in 1527 would doubtless be considered by specialist scholars today as a minor actor during the civic humanist phase of the later period of the Florentine Renaissance – indeed, if he were studied at all. Certainly, he would not merit a book such as the present one, let alone be deserving of the sturdy reputation (or notoriety) he enjoys or of the thousands of scholarly and polemical tomes that have been directed at his writings and his career.

Early readers and critics

What transpired between June 1527 and the approaching fifth centenary of his death makes for a fascinating tale in itself. During the first few decades of the sixteenth century, Machiavelli was barely known outside of Italy. His *Art of War* was read and respected, but hardly controversial. Manuscripts of his other prose works seem to have circulated for some time, and indeed in 1524 a plagiarized and carefully pruned Latin version of *The Prince*, addressed to Emperor Charles V, was published in Naples by a Pisan philosophy professor, Agostino Nifo. It seems unlikely that Machiavelli ever became aware of Nifo's act of creative theft, but when the first Italian version of *The Prince* appeared in print in May 1532, its editor, Bernardo di Giunta, complained of the act of Latin plagiarism. The *Discourses* had been published in Rome in 1531 and the *History of Florence* in 1532 (all by the papal printer, Antonio Blando!), from autograph or reliable manuscripts, so that within five years after Machiavelli's demise his major prose works were available. Most of the earliest known readers of these works (including Machiavelli's close friend Francesco Guicciardini, who wrote an unfinished commentary on the *Discourses*) were sympathetic, if critical, in their attitude.

Machiavelli's reputation altered much for the worse at the hands of the English Cardinal Reginald Pole, who in 1539 included an extensive attack on *The Prince* in his *Apologia* addressed to Charles V. Pole's tract was highly polemical and even incendiary: *The Prince* is described as a work composed by 'the finger of Satan' attached to the human hand of one Niccolò Machiavelli. Pole seems to have initiated a tradition of anti-Machiavellian writing during the middle of the sixteenth century that culminated in the inclusion of the entire corpus of Machiavelli on the papal Index of Prohibited Books in 1559. Yet even with the hostility evinced by Pole and others, as well as the official Catholic ban, the flow of publication of Machiavelli's work hardly ceased. Between 1527 and the centenary of his death, more than 150 editions, adaptations, and translations of his work entered into print, of which greater than half occurred after 1559. One suspects that the Roman prohibition only drew wider attention to Machiavelli's writings, especially outside of Italy. In particular, Machiavelli's major prose treatises were broadly disseminated and enthusiastically received in

France and England during the second half of the sixteenth century.

The publication history of translated versions of the main Machiavellian works produced a mixed legacy. Machiavelli's name was implicated in the events surrounding the St Bartholomew's Day Massacre of August 1572, in which tens of thousands of French Protestants (known as Huguenots) were killed by royal troops, initiating a period of bloody religious wars. While it seems implausible that a conscious plan modeled on Machiavelli's doctrines lay behind these events, many Huguenots suspected otherwise. This suspicion crystallized with the publication of Innocent Gentillet's tract *Contre-Machiavel* in 1576. Perhaps the most influential and powerful attack to appear in the sixteenth century, Gentillet's book, the first study dedicated entirely to the Florentine author, is credited with burnishing the stereotype of Machiavelli as the supreme counselor of violence and evil in politics, the inventor of 'not a Politicke, but a Tyrannical science'. For Gentillet, *The Prince* afforded the key to understanding Machiavelli's teachings, and the rest of the corpus was read through the prism of that volume. The ensuing stereotype of the 'murderous Machiavelli' spread throughout Europe along with the dispersion of the Huguenots following the Massacre (Gentillet himself had settled in Geneva, where he composed his polemic). This image was only reinforced by the numerous editions and reissues of the *Contre-Machiavel* published in the following years. Yet, somewhat ironi-cally, the unintended effect of Gentillet's sustained critique, as of the earlier papal condemnation, was the intensification of inter-est in Machiavelli and the continued printing and distribution of his major works. The more pointedly and vociferously Machiavelli was reviled, it seems, the greater grew his fame.

Nor did Machiavelli entirely lack defenders in the century or so after his death. This was the period in which the doctrine of 'Reason of State' was emerging throughout Europe, that is, the position that governments could legitimately employ their sovereign power however necessity demanded in order to maintain public order and control. The authors associated with the 'Reason of State' argument (both Catholics and Protestants) often did not cite Machiavelli directly by name, but they certainly knew his writings and borrowed from them in developing their own ideas. Indeed, even strong advocates of Machiavelli's political insights, such as the German Caspar Schoppe in the early seventeenth century, took care not to mention him explicitly or to make their references highly elliptical. Similarly, Machiavelli continued to be an important source for historical and military purposes, again largely without attribution. Machiavelli thus became a somewhat spectral figure in a vast body of early modern literature, a ghost who hovered behind much of the political writing of the age but whose overt authority could not be invoked. When the English republican James Harrington, in his mid-seventeenth-century treatise *The Commonwealth of Oceana*, lamented that Machiavelli's 'books are neglected', his remark pertains less to the substance of the Florentine's thought than to the ability to refer to him as the source. Harrington himself did much to reverse this trend by openly praising Machiavelli, especially in regard to his *Discourses*, which provided a major inspiration for the republican regime imagined in *Oceana*. By the latter 1600s, Machiavelli was undergoing a thorough rehabilitation in some circles, even as he continued to be an object of revulsion and loathing among others.

In sum, the story of the early reception of Machiavelli does not constitute a monolithic or unilinear narrative. He was read from multiple perspectives and was judged (positively or negatively) according to a number of divergent standards. This situation continues into the present day. There exists little agreement about how to understand, let alone evaluate, the teachings of Machiavelli both in their original meaning and in their implications for political theory in current times. As suggested in the preface to this volume, the reason for this stems mainly from the highly dichotomous character of his leading ideas as expressed throughout his corpus. Machiavelli saw alternative and sometimes quite opposite solutions to the cosmological, psychological, military, and institutional dilemmas he confronted, and he never entirely resolved them to his own satisfaction. Hence, we encounter the very fragmented state of his legacy, which shall be surveyed briefly below.

Later interpretations

Perhaps the most obvious question with which to begin is that of whether Machiavelli was in fact a 'Machiavellian' (a term invented in the sixteenth century). It should be evident that there are many twists and turns involved in giving any feasible answer. If Machiavellianism connotes crass opportunism in the name of acquiring or maintaining power for its own sake, then Machiavelli does not deserve to be tarred with the brush of his own name. He evinced throughout his life an unwavering commitment to certain firm beliefs about standards for evaluating political affairs, which he was able to articulate and to defend cogently. Machiavelli was sufficiently convinced of the superiority of republican rule, insofar as he held that there were good reasons – practical as well as moral – to endorse self-government in preference to princely regimes. Moreover, he rejected any uses of power that were likely to produce hatred on the part of the people, regarding such means to be evil as well as self-defeating. Yet Machiavelli was prepared to admit of degrees in the judgment of political affairs. He declined, unlike Plato or other ancient or modern philosophers, to insist that a single type of government or constitutional order afforded the best or only 'true' form of politics. Rather, Machiavelli made more fine-grained distinctions, so that he was prepared to countenance types of political conduct that others rejected out of hand on moralistic grounds. He doubted human capacities for achieving ideal results, but he did not descend into the basest sort of cynicism. He balanced his negative evaluation of what human beings could achieve as individuals with a chastened optimism about what they might be able to accomplish collectively. Hence, Machiavelli could without contradiction accept the necessities that accompanied inferior forms of government such as principalities without dismissing the aspirations of republican regimes to provide liberty for their citizens.

The ambivalent aspects of Machiavelli's thought and writings in turn licensed the wide variety of fates for his reputation long after his lifetime. On the one hand, his supposed immoralism was reviled by a vast array of critics, including not least the Prussian crown prince Frederick, who composed a treatise called the *Anti-Machiavel* in the middle of the eighteenth century. As stated above, Machiavelli was both lauded and condemned for his supposed formulation of the doctrine of 'Reason of State'. He has been assigned responsibility for formulating a version of 'political realism' that accepted the validity of justifications for the state to act instrumentally for its own good, without regard for constraints of religious piety and moral convention. Even today, one of the most common schools of interpretation concerning Machiavelli depicts him as a 'teacher of evil' and proponent of tyranny who not merely rejected the role of ethical considerations in politics, but even reveled in the use of cruelty, treachery, and violence as worthy political techniques.

On the other hand, the republican dimension of Machiavelli's thought enjoys an equally strong reputation. Jean-Jacques Rousseau remarked in Book 3 of *On the Social Contract* that 'Machiavelli's *Prince* is the book of republicans', since 'while pretending to teach lessons to Kings, he taught great lessons to peoples'. Rousseau characterized Machiavelli as 'an honest man and a good citizen', who 'was forced during the oppression of his fatherland to disguise his love of freedom'. Rousseau supported his republican interpretation of *The Prince* by referring to its apparent contradictions with his other writings, such as the *Discourses* and the *History of Florence*. Likewise, the diffusion of Machiavelli's republican thought has been observed throughout the Atlantic world and, specifically, in the ideas that guided the framers of the American constitution regarding the inevitability of factions and the construction of a system of checks and balances. The *Discourses* has received attention at least as wide as *The Prince* during recent times, being afforded commendation and praise as an antidote to the view of Machiavelli as a 'murderous' author.

At the same time, there has been deep dispute about the specific nature of the republican theory that Machiavelli propounded. According to some interpretations, his republicanism is of a civic humanist variety whose roots are to be found in classical antiquity. Machiavelli is therefore regarded to be an important source for conveying a political tradition with a considerable pedigree. His recurrent strong praise for the civic virtues associated with the Roman Republic, in particular, seems to support such an understanding of his work. But other readers have stressed the profound modernity of the intellectual substance of Machiavellian republicanism, hence judging the *Discourses* to represent a complete break with earlier conceptions of republican government. On this view, the values that Machiavelli attributed to the ancient world would not have been recognized as such by either the theorists or the politicians of antiquity. In particular, classical political ideas were imbued with an emphasis on the attainment of harmony and balance as the keys to attaining liberty, whereas Machiavelli lauds conflict and contention. His beloved Romans advocated peace and order; he judged the main elements of their public life to derive from turbulent class divisions. The issue is not whether Machiavelli's historical reconstruction of Rome in fact affords a more accurate interpretation of the reasons for that city's emergence as the preeminent military and political force of the ancient world. Rather, the point is that his conception of the institutional and personal qualities that made the Roman Republic great has a decidedly non-Roman and very modern cast.

Such disagreement about the character of Machiavelli's republicanism raises the broader problem of his relationship to his intellectual sources and historical context, which poses the question of his 'originality'. Cases have been made for and against Machiavelli's political morality, his conception of the state, his religious views, and many other features of his work as forming the distinctive basis for the 'originality' of his contribution. Machiavelli certainly encouraged this impression, repeatedly insisting upon his own innovations in contrast with the views of his predecessors. In particular, he foregrounds his own 'realism' and 'usefulness' in comparison with authors who 'have fancied for themselves republics and principalities that have never been seen or known to exist in reality' (P, 15; CW, p. 57). He reinforces this impression repeatedly by proffering criticisms of both conventional and contemporary writers who uphold a moralism that he judges impractical and politically naive. Yet it remains an open question the extent to which we ought to share Machiavelli's exaggerated claims for his own novelty. He seldom mentions by name those from whom he seeks to distance himself. In many instances, moreover, precedents can indeed be identified for the supposed innovations that he ascribes to his own work. In sum, few firm conclusions can be drawn about how original Machiavelli truly is. A more reasonable judgment is that Machiavelli was effectively trapped between innovation and tradition in a way that generated internal conceptual tensions within his thought as a whole and even within individual texts. Such historical ambiguity permits Machiavelli's readers to make equally convincing cases for contradictory claims about his fundamental stance without appearing to commit egregious violence to his doctrines.

None of this is to say that Machiavelli was fundamentally inconsistent. Rather, the apparently conflicting features of his thought may be credited to his attempt to innovate by means of looking back to widely known historical examples and genres of political writing, while at the same time to draw different conclusions from the commonplace expectations of his audience. Thus, he could not avoid the incorporation of important elements of precisely the conventions he was challenging. For example, in chapter 18 of *The Prince*, he seems to advise would-be rulers to prepare themselves for the commission of immorality in order to succeed, yet he never explicitly proposes (as many have supposed) that evil actions are worthy or meritorious in themselves. Indeed, in chapter 8, speaking of Agathocles, he says precisely the opposite, namely, that 'his outrageous cruelty and inhumanity together with his countless wicked acts do not permit him to be honored among the noblest men' (P, 8; CW, p. 36). Political success may, for a time, accompany the use of such techniques, but this is due to their suitability under the circumstances, not the inherent value of the actions themselves. It may seem that Machiavelli embraces a contradiction, but this is perhaps best understood as a reflection of the fact that he cannot bring himself to reverse totally the standard moral convictions of his day. In spite of his repeated assertions of his own originality, his careful attention to preexisting traditions meant that he was never fully able to escape his intellectual confines. Thus, Machiavelli might best be understood as simultaneously 'original' and 'conventional', as both an 'ancient' and a 'modern', a thinker of great vision who still remained deeply imbedded in and indebted to the context within which he wrote.

An especially clear example of Machiavelli's ambivalent relationship with his intellectual and political milieu emerges from an examination of his concept of the state. Machiavelli has been credited with formulating for the first time the 'modern concept of the state', understood in the sense of an impersonal form of rule possessing a monopoly of coercive authority within a fixed territorial boundary. Certainly, the term *lo stato* appears widely in Machiavelli's writings, especially in *The Prince*, in connection with the acquisition and application of power in a coercive sense, which renders its meaning distinct from the Latin term *status* (condition or station) from which it is derived. Moreover, Machiavelli's influence in shaping the early modern debates surrounding 'Reason of State' suggests that he was received by his near-contemporaries as a theorist of the state.

Yet a careful reading of Machiavelli's use of *lo stato* in *The Prince* and elsewhere does not fully support this conclusion. Machaivelli's 'state' remains a personal patrimony, a possession more in line with the medieval conception of *dominium* as the foundation of rule. (*Dominium* is a Latin term that may be translated with equal force as 'private property' and as 'political dominion'.) Thus, the 'state' is literally owned by whichever prince happens to have control of it. Moreover, the character of governance is determined by the personal qualities and traits of the ruler – hence, Machiavelli's emphasis on *virtù* as indispensable for the prince's success. These aspects of his deployment of *lo stato* mitigate against the 'modernity' of the idea in his writings. Machiavelli is at best a transitional figure in the process by which the language of the state emerged in early modern Europe. The idea of a stable constitutional regime that reflects the tenor of modern political thought (and practice) is nowhere to be seen in Machiavelli's conception of princely government.

Machiavelli today

To conclude that Machiavelli's thought does not represent a radical break with the past or with its immediate context might seem to imply that Machiavelli is outdated or irrelevant to twenty-first-century concerns. Nothing could further from the truth. Rather, his writings continue to offer to the contemporary reader considerable challenges and quandaries that persist as endemic to politics. Most obviously, Machiavelli provides a serious caution about the dangers of searching for permanent or final solutions to political problems. His conception of fortune warns us that circumstances are constantly changing in the realm of politics; matters that seem settled and fixed for all times can and do change rapidly and in ways that are beyond the capacity of human beings to foresee and forestall. Not too many years ago, the existence of two polarized and monolithic political blocks – one built around the United States, the other around Russia – seemed to be an enduring source of global identity and conflict. Almost overnight, the Soviet empire disappeared and left the United States as the sole hegemonic force, the single 'superpower', whereupon many pundits and intellectuals proclaimed some version of the 'end of history' thesis, according to which the liberal-capitalist system had been proven superior and ultimately victorious. Yet only a few years later, the rise of Islamic religious fundamentalism generated a new set of political conditions that had been entirely overlooked and unappreciated. There is talk now of the decline of supposedly unrivalled American hegemony and the emergence of a multi-polar or even Islamic-centered organization of international power relations. Examples of rapid change in public affairs could be multiplied many times over. Machiavelli, of course, would by no means be surprised. The force of his analysis might be summarized in simple terms: expect the unexpected! Since individual leaders, and even political collectivities, generally fall back upon the presumption that the future will resemble the past and present, human institutions are generally unprepared for such extreme changes of circumstance. The wheel of the goddess *Fortuna* spins in the twenty-first century no less than in the sixteenth, and men remain now as then entirely unprepared to respond to the demands of the times.

The dual lessons of the inevitability of change and of the incapacity of human actors to accept this (despite the evidence of history as well as observable experience) might seem to suggest the futility of making any sort of generalizations about politics, indeed, a stoical acceptance of whatever fortune brings. Yet Machiavelli would not endorse quietism either. Even if he did not imagine that individuals would ever be able to acquire the ensemble of traits that he summarizes by the word *virtù*, he teaches us that well-designed political institutions (especially those of a populist, republican sort) hold out the promise of staving off some of the otherwise inscrutable consequences of fortune. A single leader, constrained by the fixities of human psychology, will never be as capable to govern as a diverse and pluralistic community that contains many different types of personality. To be sure, Machiavelli was no advocate of democracy in its more unrestrained versions, since he feared it would lead to anarchy (and licentiousness) rather than to civic-minded liberty. But he defended a vision of republican government that, at minimum, supports the political efficacy of a system that circulates elites and finds ways to hold them accountable to a popular will. While such a system, in his view, might be noisy and clamoring (and perhaps extremely divided and conflictual on occasion), it also stood the best chance of yielding a combination of appropriate leadership and wise discretion. The security afforded by well-ordered monarchies (of which there are very few) is desirable, but the liberty intrinsic to the well-ordered republic is to be valued more greatly.

The way in which Machiavelli filters his political lessons through the prisms of historical analysis and experiential evidence also conveys an important message. His approach to politics clearly eschews a purely deductive, philosophical method in favor of observations about specific events from the past and recent times. This has often been taken to reflect a strongly pragmatic streak in his thought, a conclusion that Machiavelli encourages by insisting upon his single-minded concern with 'reality' and his aim 'to write something useful' according to 'the truth of the matter as facts show it rather than any fanciful notion' (P, 15; CW, p. 57). Yet we must realize that Machiavelli's empirical generalizations about political affairs rest upon the central foundation of his theory of human nature. By studying carefully the historical record, we can apply what we learn to current and future events, insofar as human beings are basically unchanging across time. Thus, as Machiavelli remarks in the *Discourses*, 'he who wishes to see what is to come should observe what has already happened, because all the affairs of the world, in every age, have their individual counterparts in ancient times. The reason for this is that since they are carried on by men, who have and always have had the same passions, of necessity the same results appear' (D, 3.43; CW, p. 521). The prologue to the *Clizia* opens with an essentially identical comment: 'If into the world the same men should come back, just as the same events come back, never would a hundred years go by in which we should not find here a second time the very same things done as now' (C, Prologue; CW, p. 823). The constancy of human nature (both generally and among individuals) permits us to employ history as a guide to our own circumstances. Conditions may indeed change in accordance with the whims of fortune, but there are a limited range of ways in which human beings react to the events that confront them, which lends a measure of predictability to the present and future. Machiavelli's method is by no means 'scientific', since science would require the sort of complete and perfect foresight into the workings of *Fortuna* that he deems impossible. Yet even without access to knowledge of the alteration of circumstances beyond human control, Machiavelli believes that our understanding of human nature and consequent modes of conduct yields considerable information about reasonable expectations concerning political affairs. The past forms a bridge to the future.

We might conclude, then, that for Machiavelli politics, and perhaps all manner of human endeavors, admit at best of provisional solutions to the problems they pose. The study of political affairs can improve our knowledge of how to conduct government, design institutions, and organize social relations, but it cannot permanently resolve the dilemmas we face. The occult forces of *Fortuna* are too fickle and complex to be grasped and controlled by acts of human intellect and will. Perhaps if, like Moses, we could enjoy privileged access to the divine plan and thus use such insight as a guide and an opportunity for action, success would be forever within human reach. But those possessing a special relationship with God are truly rare, in Machiavelli's estimation; someone who claims to enjoy divine friendship, such as the 'unarmed prophet' Savonarola, usually winds up a victim of fortune, even if he had been able for a time to convince his fellow citizens that he conversed with God (D, 1.11; CW, p. 226). By contrast, most individuals who enter into public affairs must muddle along, trying to prepare themselves for whatever unforeseen and unforeseeable circumstances are thrown into their paths. For such people, more mundane inquiries, including the study of history and the examination of the characteristics of leaders and populations, may prove useful. The lessons that these investigations teach do not ensure political success. At best, the knowledge they yield, if applied to particular conundrums, improves the likelihood that public affairs will be ordered so as to resist some of the blows of fortune. Machiavelli vacillates between a chastened optimism and a qualified pessimism regarding the extent of human powers. In the intervening five centuries since his death, his basic appraisal of political life – that flux is the norm – has not been refuted. Indeed, the events of the past five hundred years seem only to confirm the continuing wisdom and value of Machiavelli's counsels against the rush to posit permanent answers to political questions. Almost as fast as solutions are proffered – think of communism, fascism, colonialism, and the many other ideologies that have been put into practice during just the past century alone – they prove unsustainable or worse in the face of the times. Machiavelli's tentative evaluations and provisional recommendations seem eminently more sustainable than the many alternatives that have been proposed.

Select bibliography

The best available English collected edition of Machiavelli's major and minor works is edited and translated by Allan Gilbert, *Machiavelli: The Chief Works and Others*, 3 vols (Durham: Duke University Press, 1965). Gilbert's renderings, while sometimes slightly flowery, are competent and accessible. There are many other translations of Machiavelli's major prose and theatrical works, the reliability of which varies widely. Machiavelli's letters to and from friends have been collected and translated, with extremely useful critical apparatus, by James B. Aktinson and David Sices, eds, *Machiavelli and His Friends: Their Personal Correspondence* (DeKalb: Northern Illinois University Press, 1996).

Several excellent, though quite diverse, biographies have been published in English during the last few years: Sebastian De Grazia, *Machiavelli in Hell* (Princeton: Princeton University Press, 1989), which won the Pulitzer Prize for biography; Maurizio Viroli, *Niccolò's Smile: A Biography of Machiavelli* (New York: Hill and Wang, 2000); Michael White, *Machiavelli: A Man Misunderstood* (London: Little, Brown, 2004); and Ross King, *Machiavelli: Philosopher of Power* (New York: HarperCollins, 2007). I have relied on all these volumes, as well as additional specialized research, in preparing my own biographical and intellectual sketch in chapter 1. Among scholarly studies, I found particularly useful Catherine Atkinson's *Debts, Dowries, Donkeys: The Diary of Niccolò Machiavelli's Father, Messer Bernardo, in Quattrocento Florence* (Frankfurt a.M.: Peter Lang, 2002).

A masterful and much-needed study of Machiavelli's early dissemination and reception is Sydney Anglo's *Machiavelli: The First Century* (Oxford: Oxford University Press, 2005). John Pocock traces the impact of Machiavelli's republican dimensions, especially as manifested in the Anglo-American context, in *The Machiavellian Moment* (Princeton: Princeton University Press, 1975). Also illuminating is

Maurizio Viroli's *From Politics to Reason of State* (Cambridge: Cambridge University Press, 1992).

The scholarly literature on Machiavelli's thought is legion. A few of the more important, interesting and useful (and often conflicting) recent studies in English include:

Anglo, Sydney. *Machiavelli: A Dissection*. London: Paladin, 1971.

Ascoli, Albert Russell and Victoria Kahn, eds. *Machiavelli and the Discourse of Literature*. Ithaca, NY: Cornell University Press, 1993.

Baron, Hans. *The Crisis of the Early Italian Renaissance*. Princeton: Princeton University Press, 1966.

—— *In Search of Florentine Civic Humanism: Essays on the Transition from Medieval to Modern Thought*. 2 vols. Princeton: Princeton University Press, 1988.

Bock, Gisela, Quentin Skinner, and Maurizio Viroli, eds. *Machiavelli and Republicanism*. Cambridge: Cambridge University Press, 1990.

Bondanella, Peter E. *Machiavelli and the Art of Renaissance History*. Detroit: Wayne State University Press, 1973.

Chabod, Federico. *Machiavelli and the Renaissance*. Trans. David Moore. London: Bowes & Bowes, 1958.

Coby, J. Patrick. *Machiavelli's Romans: Liberty and Greatness in the Discourses on Livy*. Lanham, MD: Lexington Books, 1999.

Coyle, Martin, ed. *Niccolò Machiavelli's The Prince*. Manchester: Manchester University Press, 1995.

Femia, Joseph V. *Machiavelli Revisited*. Cardiff: University of Wales Press, 2004.

Fischer, Markus. *Well-Ordered License: On the Unity of Machiavelli's Thought*. Lanham, MD: Lexington Books, 2000.

Fleisher, Martin, ed. *Machiavelli and the Nature of Political Thought*. New York: Atheneum, 1972.

Fontana, Benedetto. *Hegemony and Power: On the Relation between Gramsci and Machiavelli*. Minneapolis: University of Minnesota Press, 1993.

Gilbert, Felix. *Machiavelli and Guicciardini: Politics and History in Sixteenth Century Florence*. New York: W.W. Norton & Co., 1984.

Godman, Peter. *From Poliziano to Machiavelli: Florentine Humanism in the High Renaissance.* Princeton: Princeton University Press, 1998.

Hankins, James, ed. *Renaissance Civic Humanism.* Cambridge: Cambridge University Press, 2000.

Hörnqvist, Mikael. *Machiavelli and Empire.* Cambridge: Cambridge University Press, 2004.

Hulliung, Mark. *Citizen Machiavelli.* Princeton: Princeton University Press, 1983.

Kahn, Victoria. *Machiavellian Rhetoric: From the Counter-Reformation to Milton.* Princeton: Princeton University Press, 1994.

Landon, William J. *Politics, Patriotism and Language: Niccolò Machiavelli's 'Secular Patria' and the Creation of an Italian National Identity.* New York: Peter Lang Publishing, 2005.

Mansfield, Harvey. *Machiavelli's Virtue.* Chicago: University of Chicago Press, 1996.

Najemy, John M. *Between Friends: Discourses of Power and Desire in the Machiavelli–Vittori Letters of 1513–1515.* Princeton: Princeton University Press, 1993.

Parel, Anthony J. *The Machiavellian Cosmos.* New Haven: Yale University Press, 1992.

Pitkin, Hanna Fenichel. *Fortune Is a Woman: Gender and Politics in the Thought of Niccolò Machiavelli.* Berkeley: University of California Press, 1984.

Prezzolini, Giuseppe. *Machiavelli.* New York: Farrar, Straus & Giroux, 1967.

Rebhorn, Wayne A. *Foxes and Lions: Machiavelli's Confidence Men.* Ithaca, NY: Cornell University Press, 1988.

Skinner, Quentin. *Machiavelli.* Oxford: Oxford University Press, 1981.

Strauss, Leo. *Thoughts on Machiavelli.* Chicago: University of Chicago Press, 1958.

Sullivan, Vickie B. *Machiavelli's Three Romes: Religion, Human Liberty, and Politics Reformed.* DeKalb: Northern Illinois University Press, 1996.

Vatter, Miguel E. *Between Form and Event: Machiavelli's Theory of Political Freedom.* Boston: Kluwer Academic Publishers, 2000.

Viroli, Maurizio. *Machiavelli*. New York: Oxford University Press, 1998.

Von Vacano, Diego A. *The Art of Power: Machiavelli, Nietzsche, and the Making of Aesthetic Political Theory*. Lanham, MD: Lexington Books, 2007.

Index

A Beginner's Guide to Anarchism

In this clear and penetrating study, Ruth Kinna goes right to the heart of the ideology, explaining the influences that have shaped anarchism, and the tactics and strategies that anarchists have used to bring about their goals.

978-1-85168-370-4
£9.99/ $14.95

"Kinna is an ideal guide and has written an exemplary work of clarification and explanation. This book deserves to be read very widely." **David Goodway** – Senior Lecturer In Political Theory, University of Leeds

"A valuable contribution to our understanding of this much misunderstood philosophy." **Howard Zinn** – Author of *A People's History Of The United States*

RUTH KINNA is Lecturer in Politics at Loughborough University, UK. She is the author of *William Morris: The Art of Socialism* and co-editor of the journal *Anarchist Studies*. Her research focuses on socialism and anarchism in 19th century Britain.

Browse further titles at
www.oneworld-publications.com

A Beginner's Guide to Democracy

David Beetham offers new insights into the role of the citizen and how large corporations affect democracy as well as contemplating the future of democracy in the developed and developing worlds.

978-1-85168-363-5
£9.99/ $14.95

"Beetham's book should stimulate anyone, beginner or expert, who is interested in the survival and renewal of democracy in the era of globalization." **Peter Singer** – Author of *The President Of Good And Evil: Taking George Bush Seriously*

"A strong and shrewd mixture of analysis and polemic…If more was not to come, I would call this the author's crowning achievement." **Sir Bernard Crick** – Advisor on citizenship to the UK government

DAVID BEETHAM is Professor Emeritus of Politics at the University of Leeds, a Fellow of the Human Rights Centre at the University of Essex, and Associate Director of the UK Democratic Audit.

Browse further titles at
www.oneworld-publications.com

A Beginner's Guide to Marx

Andrew Collier breathes new life into the achievements of Karl Marx, arguing that his work is still of vital relevance in today's global climate of inequality. Covering all the elements of Marxist thought from his early writings to his masterpiece, *Das Kapital*, Collier probes the apparent inconsistencies in Marx's work and reclaims him as a philosopher and political theorist.

978-1-85168-534-9
£9.99/ $14.95

"A superb new introduction to Marx's thought. Demonstrates why Marxian thought continues to find an audience in the twenty-first century." **Mark Rupert** - Professor of Political Science, Syracuse University

"An engaging and lively introduction to Marx's life and work." **Terrell Carver** - Professor of Political Theory, University of Bristol.

ANDREW COLLIER is is Professor of Philosophy at the University of Southampton. He is the author of several books including *Christianity and Marxism* and *In Defence of Objectivity.*

A Beginner's Guide to Medieval Philosophy

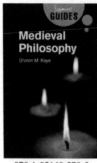

In this fast-paced, enlightening guide, Sharon M. Kaye takes us on a whistle-stop tour of medieval philosophy, revealing the debt it owes to Aristotle and Plato, and showing how medieval thought is still inspiring philosophers and thinkers today.

978-1-85168-578-3
£9.99/ $14.95

"Beautifully written and wonderfully accessible. Discussing all the major thinkers and topics of the period, Kaye's volume does exactly what it should." **William Irwin** – Professor of Philosophy, King's College Pennsylvania and Editor of *The Blackwell Philosophy and Pop Culture Series*

"Simultaneously entices students into and prepares them for the riches of the abundant literature that lies ready for their exploration." **Martin Tweedale** – Professor Emeritus of Medieval Philosophy, University of Alberta

SHARON M. KAYE is Associate Professor of Philosophy at John Carroll University. She is the author of *On Ockham* and *On Augustine*.

Browse further titles at
www.oneworld-publications.com